BARRY SHEENE

AND MY PART IN HIS DOWNFALL

IAN BURGESS

Typeset in Palatino

Editing, design, typesetting and publishing by UK Book Publishing

www.ukbookpublishing.com

ISBN: 978-1-913179-83-0

BARRY SHEENE

AND MY PART IN HIS DOWNFALL

For my mother, Joan Burgess, who sadly passed away in November 2017

With thanks and appreciation to my friend Dan Sager, Mr Motorcycling PR in the UK, without whose help and guidance this would not be as good as it is.

INTRODUCTION

L ife gets in the way, I've been thinking about writing this book for many years. More than 25 years in fact. After all I left Suzuki GB in April 1983, having been made redundant out of the blue, I suppose it always is out of the blue, and while Suzuki GB Managing Director Denys Rohan was giving me the bad news in his office Barry came walking in sporting his usual big grin. He slapped me on the back and told me I'd won the little bet we had taken just a few days earlier at the French Grand Prix.

'Not now Barry' were the only words Denys could muster. He cut Barry short who, by now, looked very confused. Barry left the room as did I a few moments later to find Barry leaning against the wall outside. I told him what had happened as we both walked off along the top corridor together. I was stunned by the news and didn't really know what to do or who to talk to. I had given my all to Suzuki, seven days a week and with total enthusiasm through thick and thin.

But this book isn't just about Barry, Suzuki GB and the many good times I had there. It's also about my journey into bike racing, as a sidecar passenger, BEMSEE (British Motorcycle Racing Club) and becoming very involved with club and national racing and the great riders I got to know along the way.

Keith Huewen, Conor Brennan, Gary Lingham, Damon Hill are just a few of the names who shone in what was arguably the best period in bike racing in the UK. Races came thick and fast weekend after weekend. We all assembled at the circuit of the week, chewed the fat, played tricks and told outrageous stories. The laughter never stopped except when someone went crashing down the track. Then when the crasher gave the thumbs up from the track side or the Red Cross ambulance, we all laughed out loud once more.

In this book I am going to spill the beans on certain events and tell the inside story of what it was like to be catapulted from part time PR man for BEMSEE whilst working at MCN in their London advertising office, to becoming Suzuki GB PR manager to follow in the heavy footsteps of Andy Foulkes who coincidently I had worked with at MCN. There were many ups and downs along the Suzuki GB road. The ins and outs and the amazing characters who worked there and who made every day so much fun and completely unpredictable. Riders such as Graeme Crosby, Randy Mamola, Paul Iddon, Mark Boughton, Rob McElnea and of course John Newbold all came and went during my time at SGB.

I'm also going to tell the truth about Barry, warts and all. That truth has possibly never been told before and I do it not to besmirch his character but to show how the mega super star who was our brightest and most famous son at the time, and perhaps the most influential British racer ever, was also human and as such had some foibles and faults. Sometimes it helps to know that someone who we hold so dear to our heart wasn't without issues and troubles. That truth and the observations about Barry are what has made me think long and hard about this book. Barry was my idol and hero from the first time I heard about him and watched him race in the 1974 season, and amazingly finding out that my cousin Graham was one of the first Suzuki GB mechanics to prepare bikes and engines for him in the old workshops at Beddington Lane, Wallington.

They say never meet your heroes, well in Barry I did and many times. I felt privileged to be friends with him, as much as anyone could be and certainly when Barry was with you he would help and get stuff moving. He had great energy and power to influence people. That's probably why he never had an agent or manager and did all his own deals and negotiations. But he also had a darker side. It's this darker side that I explore a little here in the book plus I shed some thoughts and light on some of the rumours that were circulating about him.

So, if you're reading this book, I thank you for buying it and hope you enjoy the ride. And just for good measure I must draw your attention to the one book you must have in your collection about Suzuki. It's called *Team Suzuki*, was written by Ray Battersby and first published in 1982. Ray was what I would call the Suzuki GB technical director though he is far more humble in his own description. The book is sadly out of print as far as I know but copies are available on ebay. It is a unique mix of historical insight, first hand observation, technical analysis and a darn good yarn about the journey Suzuki had through the years, from the very early exploits in

GPs with Ernst Degner, through the Barry years and into the early eighties with Randy and Croz. I can't recommend this book highly enough and whatever it costs will be money well spent.

Finally I need to say thanks to a few people out loud and some anonymous mates too. Keith Huewen was always close by before and during my times at Suzuki and quite astutely observed, when I told him of this book, that 'you were in a quite uniquely placed position to see things from a different perspective'. Then there was Paul Iddon, and Anita who was Mark Boughton's girlfriend when he was at Suzuki GB. They all deserve a mention for giving me their time and views from the period. Plus of course there a few people who freely gave of their memories but didn't want a mention. Thanks to one and all.

Ian Burgess

THE EARLY DAYS

I was born and brought up in Kent and had my first motorcycle accident at about the age of twelve or thirteen. In the gravel alleyway which ran between the old and new houses at the back of our street someone had brought an old Lambretta 200 to muck around on. I am fairly certain this was my first ever ride on a bike. There were a group of teenage lads all taking turns to go up and down the alleyway. Being offered a ride was too much to turn down and not having a clue what to do just hopped on, revved it up and lost control within fifty yards ploughing through the wooden garden fence of one of our neighbours. Needless to say I wasn't wearing a helmet. Picking myself up in the vegetable patch of Mrs Pearcy's garden was bad enough but finding her looking down at me with a face like thunder was an altogether different experience.

Me and my mates removed the scooter, patched up the garden and fence a little and then legged it. I spent the next hour or so being attended to by my mum who carefully picked the splinters out of me one by one and then used TCP to sort out the scrapes.

A couple of years later with a decent paying Saturday job under my control the world changed when Yamaha launched the FS1E.

My Saturday job was a little bit special and very hard work. I got the job of first assistant BOY in the tea stall opposite the entry gates to the Tower of London in Tower Hill. Each Saturday I would get up very early, never a problem for me, walk to the train station at Albany Park, and get the train to London Bridge. Then walk across the mostly empty bridge turning right into Monument Street, past the Great Fire of London tower and along to Tower Hill.

The tourists in the summertime would already be accumulating and milling around waiting for the big wooden gates, to the Tower, to be opened. The day would fly by. It was non-stop. Hundreds of customers came and went buying tea and coffee, sandwiches and rolls, over 300 cans of Coke would be sold every day. My job was to do a bit of everything and do it quickly. Every now and again Bill, the City of London and Tower of London parking warden, would come by with his very large smile and offer jellied eels or some other delicacy. It was all new to me, I quickly learned proper east end phrases and Cockney rhyming slang and I loved it too!

For this fun and education, I was rewarded with what I considered to be a good pay packet. Every Saturday I was paid £10 plus I could eat as much food as I wanted for free. Not bad eh?

The Yamaha FS1E (The Fizzy) dominated my thoughts and as I was shortly to be sixteen, I approached my dad to see if he would lend me the money to buy one which I could pay back on a weekly basis. I had about £30 saved and if I remember rightly the bike cost £217. My dad was lovely but not rich so I was somewhat doubtful he would be able to find that sort of money. Imagine my surprise and happiness when he agreed. Off we trotted to the local dealer and chose the gorgeous metallic purple one. I was in heaven.

By this time of course moped fever had struck Britain like the plague. Two stroke convoys were to be seen in nearly every town. If you didn't hear them you would certainly know they were around due to the ever present plume of blue and white oily smoke they left behind.

I left school in July 1975 and took an unexpected route. I went for two interviews and was offered both jobs. It was obvious which one to go for because whilst it offered me almost no money it came with a slot in college and a place on their new 'junior management trainee scheme'. The company was GEC Elliott Engineering in Lewisham, south east London.

Every two weeks or so they moved me into a different department of the company to learn what happened and what that department did in the larger mix of things, to get a feel and a better understanding of the pressures and directions of each and every department, even the union office which taught me very early about the loons of the left and their commitment to disruption and getting away with it. But the key for me was they paid for me to take a two year business studies diploma course. The job had its high points in that it was like the university of life. When you meet so many different people from the dull and boring to the dynamic go getters it all adds up to heady concoction which subconsciously shaped me at that young age. But it was boring. Very boring. I think I realised my days there were numbered when in year two one of the office Wallers told me how many miles he could get out of a new pair of leather soled shoes. My life had come to this, a discussion so tedious and dull with people who knew the mileage of shoe leather!

During that year, of course, Barry had gone from strength to strength, winning grand prix after grand prix and becoming World Champion. Like thousands of other young fans I was transfixed by Barry and his antics. Every Wednesday I was desperate to read MCN, the news, the grand prix results and paddock gossip. I dreamed of being inside the paddock instead of the detached position myself and millions of other bike sport fans watched from.

What I neither knew nor expected was my cousin, Graham Saunders, was one of the first employees of the new Suzuki GB company a few years earlier and was in fact responsible for Barry's early Suzuki TR500 engines and fettling. My dad, who by now was very aware of my passion for bikes and racing, told me to go and see Graham, so one Saturday on my new and very lovely blue Suzuki GT185 I set off for Thornton Heath. Graham was a cheeky chappie with a roll up and a big grin. Looking like a little skinny urchin from Oliver with a boyish face and unkempt hair he virtually lived in oil covered overalls and in his workshop. Graham liked nothing better than fiddling, tuning and re-building two stroke engines.

We got on well and formed a friendship. He told me about Barry and the racing side of things. In those days Suzuki GB was based along the Beddington Lane in Wallington near Croydon. Beddington Lane was more of an unkempt industrial estate type of location slotted in between the A23 and Croydon and Mitcham Common, where my grandparents lived, at the other end. It was grubby, flat common land a little bit desolate, and not the place to break down late at night.

My mind was quickly made up. I had to leave GEC and get a real job, one that interested me and kept me motivated and happy. During the lunch break every Wednesday I would sit back in whatever office they had put me in that week and quietly consume MCN. Cover to cover. A particular joy was the classified ad section. It contained many hundreds of small ads that could propel me into fantasy land as I browsed them dreaming of riding all the super bikes and dream machines listed there. It also contained the job section.

On one day late in 1976 I noticed a job ad tucked away in the classifieds, hidden almost, for the post of MCN classified ad department in the London office just off Fleet Street. The job ad didn't say a lot save for the fact that this was a junior post in the fast moving and exciting world of advertising. That was enough for me. My heart was racing, this was perfect and could be the job of a lifetime for me. I quickly wrote an application letter and sent it off the next day.

I was staggered a few days later to receive a reply asking me to come for an interview and to confirm by calling them for a quick chat. A week or so later I was in the MCN office Breams Buildings just off Fleet Street. Breams Buildings was a narrow street which runs parallel to Fleet Street a couple of hundred yards up Chancery lane behind the old Daily Express building and then led onto Fetter Lane and Holborn Circus which had the Daily Mirror building dominating it. Though the area was famous for its press and media connections it was also full of legal firms being that it is only a two minute walk along Fleet Street from the imposing Royal Courts of Justice.

The MCN office was on the upper floors of the building served by an amazing old lift. The type where a wrought iron sliding gate is closed and the traveller chooses the floor and presses the brass surrounded button to start the old but beautiful lift on its way.

My interview was with the London ad director Mr Keith McGhee. He was friendly and welcoming but then spent most of the rest of the interview sat at his desk holding this week's MCN up and calling out questions from behind it such that I hardly saw his face. The questions were all about bikes, makers, racing and asking me to identify types of bikes by their model number. So he would call out KH and I would reply 'Kawasaki', then he would say 'what happens of the Isle of Man?' or 'who makes the Goldwing?' All the time a steady cloud of smoke rose up from his head as he seemed to never stop smoking. In the background from behind the wall where the rest of the MCN offices were situated I could hear phones ringing, loud talking and laughter, doors closing and the general hubbub of an active and happy office. I loved it.

Keith told me that there was only one other candidate for the job and I would hear back very soon. The interview being over I was out the door and wandering back along Fleet Street to Charing Cross station to get my train home.

I did indeed hear back soon. With a job offer! MCN had the pleasure of offering me the position of classified advertising assistant. I couldn't accept fast enough and was so happy just a few weeks later to start my new career in advertising, one which would last some 40 years. GEC Elliot were far less happy having given me a free college course and support which they hoped would lead to a long payback working for them.

The MCN office was as fast paced as I had expected along with vicious office banter and the 'Rubber Duck' which was hurled at anyone not looking out for it. The Rubber Duck was one of those bendy toys about 5 or 6 inches high but had had the metal wire removed from it so it wouldn't cause too much damage when it hit your face at 40mph!

Being a weekly newspaper there wasn't much time to waste. The speed at which things moved and were processed was astonishing to me and took some time to get familiar with. My immediate boss was one Andrew Foulkes a large chap with a great sense of humour and an even larger capacity for drinking. In truth I was a little wary of him because he seemed to be on the edge of madness or a breakdown. The ad team was surprisingly small being made up of Keith McGhee and his deputy Peter Archer, some ad reps who were mainly out on the road selling ads to dealers, media brokers and ad agencies, the main manufacturers were managed by Keith and Peter. Then there was June the office admin manager who seemed to be the glue that kept the office together and made it all happen. MCN as you will know is published on a Wednesday but was put together on a Monday. Every Monday one or two of the office staff would disappear at about lunchtime to get the train up to Kettering where the print works and other MCN offices were based. They would return to the office a day later with a couple of dozen of that week's paper and, it seemed to me, a huge hangover.

After just a few months in that building we were all moved to a much newer office building at the other end of Hatton Garden just a ten-minute walk away. We were based on the first floor in a bright and much more usable office space. All the other magazines in the group were also in the building. Mags such as Bike, Motorcycle Mechanics, Practical Motoring, Smash Hits! and some gardening monthly.

The other guy who I was interviewed for the classified job was Adrian Marriot, who was so well thought of at the interview that they offered him the job as MCN production assistant. Adrian was my age and a great asset to the team. His quick wit and ability to organise things really helped the paper in my view. The office had a reception desk right next to me where the public could come in and place ads. It was well used with some famous faces dropping by from time to time. Most classified ads would come in by post so each day was started with us opening hundreds of envelopes, sorting out the ad, writing up the docket for each and sticking each individual ad on its own sheet, plus we would do the cheques, cash and postal orders which came along with them. Humour, fun, drinking and practical jokes were the order of the day.

After a couple of months I was issued with my MCN official jacket with my name embroidered on the left chest. We all had them and wore them proudly at events, shows and exhibitions plus race meetings. Unfortunately, Andy Foulkes left for pastures new leaving me half in charge of the classified ad desk until a new recruit came in.

Now well established I too was sent on the Monday run up to Kettering to experience life at the print works. It was not for the faint hearted. When we got to Kettering the first stop was the main MCN office which housed the full editorial department under the direction of editor Bob Berry, the production office under the control of Bob Lineham (Mr

Steady) and the advertising office which was like a mirror image of the London one I was used to.

On one of my first trips I met one of my heroes, famous GP reporter John Brown who called everyone Ace, not sure if he even knew anyone's real name but he was a delight. I had been reading his GP reports and racing interviews for years. John was considered perhaps the best writer/journalist in the business and brought a quality of writing which delighted all who read his output. He had a way with words, was clearly respected by many in the sport and industry so much so that many riders, like Barry, would only want him to sit down with and be interviewed by.

In order to be able to do the job on a Monday night at the print works one had to be union recognised. So I had to join a Union. I chose SLADE and suitably membershipped up I was allowed onto the print floor but under strict instructions not to do or touch all manner of things. The new print works had been installed and now used the newest production technologies. Gone were the hot metal days and replaced by computer generated ads and editorial which came out as strips or sections of thick white plasticised paper. Each page was then put together on upright boards. I was given a hand drawn and stapled together mock-up of the whole paper which was about A5 sized and very chunky. All the ads were indicated by name and position on each page and it was my job to check they were on the right page in the right place and not upside down or wrong in any other way. When a page was ready it was signed off by me, a production worker and an editorial staffer. Then that page was sent for print prep and gone forever, mistakes and all. There was a lot of pressure.

This would take until maybe 10pm or later and when finished the whole staff would hit the pub in Kettering high street to be locked-in until God knows when. Those who had come up from London then stayed at the George Hotel in town to which we wandered at midnight or later.

The following morning at the breakfast table the papers were hand delivered to us for delivery back to the office in London. It was on the station platform at Kettering one Tuesday morning where I first met Geoff Aspel who was then I believe editor of the one of the trade only titles. He was a very friendly and witty man, so we would travel back down to London together. His brother Michael was the famous television presenter and BBC newsreader among many other gigs such as Crackerjack and This Is Your Life.

Having been at MCN for a while now it was decided by Peter Archer that I should be given some more responsibility. In fact they gave me two extra areas to look after. The first one was office based, the recruitment page of semi display ads. A semi display ad was a box ad and inch or two square, or bigger, which could be finished artwork and thus be designed and have a picture, logo and fancy text in it. They were considerably more expensive than a classified lineage ad but got way more page presence and thus views. The page was dominated by the extremely busy London motorcycle courier firms who were always recruiting new riders. The money a rider could make in London in them days was phenomenal. A top rider who knew London and got out of bed early could make £100 a day, or up to £25,000 a year which was big money back then. The professional riders were motivated, sorted in terms of bike and their own kit and knew how to ride fast and safe through London traffic.

There were really only two London courier firms worth working for as far as I remember. Pony Express and Mercury. It was in the first week or two of my new job responsibility that I met Mike Agostini who was one of the managers for Pony Express. Mike is nine years older than me and I am proud to say not only did we become firm friends, but that friendship has lasted to this day, over forty years!

The other job that I was given, because no one else wanted it or would take it on, was the spares classified listings. In particular the half and full-page ads for Myers Motors and Vic Sampson who listed bike parts in their ads, hundreds of them. Peter Archer, the MCN ad manager told me the only practical way to handle this was to visit these two guys' shops in south London and sit down with them to update and edit the previous weeks' advert. It was long and tedious work made bearable by the fact that both of them were really nice and friendly, and also close to each other on the south circular road; Myers Motors near Forest Hill and Vic Sampson just up the road at Dulwich.

I was really quite naïve in them days and this world of used spare bike parts was at best murky and really quite a frightening eye opener for me. I would go and see Rob Myers on a Saturday morning. He had a shop front right on the south circular which sold parts over the counter and some bikes and cars from a showroom in the same building. Rob was big, muscular and had an air about him that meant business. He had that 'don't fuck with me' demeanour. We would sit in his office where the position of his large desk meant he had his back to the wall. In that wall was a small window partially covered by a table napkin style curtain.

A brew was delivered by one of his staff and the door was shut. We would then go through the full page ad, line by line inserting text and removing other parts. Every now and again I would say 'what's one of those Rob?' referring to an engine or bike part that I didn't know. Rob would smile, stand up and say 'come on I'll show you', he would then lead on out of the office and into the warehouse behind the shop which was literally full to the rafters with thousands and thousands of bikes parts, and mechanics breaking bikes up for parts at the back. I never asked where all these parts came from because I didn't want to know the answer. Some of course came from auctions, insurance companies would also sell right-offs to Rob but that surely didn't account for all these parts.

This arrangement for me to visit every week or two worked well and we honed our time together so it became quite a smooth and efficient operation. I liked Rob a lot. He was always polite and friendly and made time for my visit.

On one Saturday he was a bit wound up and slightly agitated, short tempered and probably didn't want me there. He was trying to be nice and polite as per normal but something wasn't right. Every few minutes he would turn around and glance over his shoulder through the small hatch type window behind him. He was hurrying through the list and wasn't prepared to repeat himself much which meant I had to get it all down without errors and move on at a pace that wasn't helpful. At one point he stopped, looked through the window and then said 'I might have to shoot out in a moment Ian. Got a problem to sort'.

A couple of minutes later he checked the window once more and then in an instant shot to his feet, cleared the desk in one leap and ran out through the shop onto the wide pavement in front of the shop. I sat there in shock because I could see through the little window and out to the pavement. Rob was knocking seven shades of shit out of a guy about his age and build. They were going for it but clearly Rob had the upper hand. There was no shouting and yelling, no threats, just a street fight, going toe to toe. It was hard and brutal. I couldn't believe my eyes. As quick as it started it stopped and Rob came back inside the shop and back into his office. He had red marks on his face and hands, was shaking and very very wound up.

He sat down and composed himself and then said 'I'm sorry about that Ian. It was something that needed sorting out. I've been waiting for that bloke to appear all week. I've got a problem with him and his family. Anyway where were we?' As calm as you like he settled into what we were doing just ten minutes before.

I didn't say a word and almost as if nothing had happened, we carried on finishing the ad. After which I quickly put my stuff away stood up and got my helmet and jacket and then asked him who the guy was. Rob explained there are two families who dominate the area, his and the Steadmans. The guy was a Steadman.

A few months later, on one of my Saturday visits I went into Rob's office to find a guy sitting in one of the chairs in front of Rob's desk. Rob wasn't there so I said hello to the bloke who was about 25 I would guess. He was pleasant to me but the obvious thing was that he had a pair of metal crutches and was missing the lower part of his right leg. The stump was on show but wrapped up in bandages. He told me Rob wouldn't be long but to sit down and wait. I assumed the guy was a customer who had had a bad motorcycle accident. So I asked him about it. The guy shot me a look and said 'no mate not a bike accident. I had it shot off. I was walking past here one afternoon and a Jaguar crept up alongside me, the window came down and shotgun came out. Bang! I was down and lost my leg. It would be an understatement to say I was shocked. This was like gangland London in the sixties with the Krays and the Richardsons battling over the lucrative parts of London's underworld control.

I didn't really know what to say to this poor guy, he was still in pain as the incident had only happened a few weeks earlier. Rob then came back into the office said hello and introduced the guy as one of the Steadman family! So a few weeks ago they were sworn enemies and now apparently all was ok between them. This was a world which to be honest made me very scared, these were people I didn't mix with normally and clearly you don't want to get into an argument with.

The guy got up and left the office saying goodbye to me and Rob. I must have looked shocked but Rob smoothed it all over by telling me that the two families had sorted out the issues and had joined forces to keep other groups from pushing into their manor. It was another world to me, an education that I didn't know I wanted or needed.

You can imagine my surprise when I got to know Vic Sampson, the other bike spares breaker, up in Dulwich. He operated from his flat and a whole line of lock up garages just across the road. Vic, though very nice to me, was even harder than Rob. He had short very black cropped hair and noticeably his mouth didn't open much when he spoke or was eating. Vic was thick set mostly it seemed with muscle and had a slight twitch.

In one of his lock-ups he showed me a racing sidecar outfit. A few weeks later, after we had got to know each other better Vic asked me if I would like to passenger for him. Before I knew it I said 'yes' and we were at the old air force base on Thorney Island next to Hayling Island which in turn is next to Portsmouth. The outfit Vic had was powered by a 750 Yamaha two stroke engine, I think it was an OW29 but it might have been a later engine. They were brutal and as a total beginner Vic decided I should be schooled in the art, or madness of a passenger.

The was a club event that weekend on the runways of the old air base. Flat and very fast. We ran the engine up, I hopped on wearing my old one piece leathers and hung on for dear life. What happened next cannot be explained properly. Unless you have actually ridden in one of these sidecar outfits you cannot imagine the way they take off, shaking and gaining speed like a fighter jet. They are incredible but brutal. I was being flung all over the place and by the end of that afternoon I could hardly stand up. I was so banged up and covered in bruises I literally could not pull my leathers off.

Over the weeks and months I got to know Vic a lot better. We had a laugh and he showed a very generous side to his nature. We raced at Brands, Mallory, Lyddon and one or two others but I was rubbish really. Vic always had a wad of cash with him. I asked him once why he had so much cash on him. He answered that cash was king and he never went anywhere without £800 in his pocket. Showing my naivety I asked him if he thought that was dangerous, that he might get mugged. His answer was simple and said with a little grin 'well they can try'.

Vic had been in the British army and then in some sort of mercenary unit, fighting in the Belgian Congo. It was obvious to me he had been around the block and nothing much frightened him. I liked Vic and we got along well but my racing days were numbered. Our final outing was at the famous Chimay circuit in Belgium. I'll go into this event much more later as it turned into something altogether different and involved Barry and his dad Franco.

In the mean-time life at MCN was good. It was a good team in the London office. It was fast paced, with loads of beer to ease the pain of long hours and we often had bikes supplied by the manufacturers which we could jump on for a weekend or so. Life was good.

BEMSEE, ME AND
THE EARLY YEARS

In order to go racing with Vic I had to have an ACU licence. I knew nothing much about getting one but after a few phone calls and a visit to the London office I managed to get a basic racing licence. The next thing to do, so I was told by Vic, was to join BEMSEE, the British Motorcycle Racing Club. I think BEMSEE is the oldest bike racing club in the UK and is still going strong today. They have a great website with loads of info on their history, famous events in the past and all the details on racing today.

In them days the club was based in Croydon and run by the famous or infamous Bill Rose ably assisted by Barbara. Most of their events were at Brands Hatch and Snetterton and included the Hutchinson 100 which was run the opposite way around Brands. Famous alumni of the club of course included Barry plus many many more. In fact there would be very few riders who didn't race in a BEMSEE event or the whole season.

Bill Rose, if you had never met him, would be difficult to believe was real. In today's society of snowflakes and the permanently deeply offended he would no doubt leave a swathe of crying buffoons in his wake. He was larger than life, very outspoken and never spoke at normal levels, he seemed to always shout. He had a large booming voice and when Bill was in the building everyone knew it. He was quite tall as I recall and always wore an oversized double-breasted suit. I don't know if he and Barbara were married or even at item, but together they ran the club like a military operation. Things ran well and if someone got in their way and cocked things up woe betide them!

I must have originally met Bill when racing with Vic at Brands Hatch but I don't remember when we first had a proper chat. He found out I worked at MCN in the ad department and maybe I took a booking for one of their race event ads, I am not certain. Bill looked old. He was probably of that generation that looked old even when they were only in their forties. I was in my early twenties by now and Bill seemed to be as old as my granddad.

I had been going to Brands to watch club races for some years. Brands was less than half an hour from my home in Bexley, Kent, so it was easy to hop on the bike and spend an afternoon or whole weekend there watching great racing. By now with my MCN jacket I could always get a pit pass and I knew a lot of the club racing lads.

Bill and I started to chat about the club one day at Brands. We seemed to get along well and I found that far from him being the attack dog I expected he was a very hard working and efficient man with an approach to his work and the club that was passionate and borderline obsessive. He really believed in the club being the starting point for many a famous racer and just wanted everything organised to the best of his and Barbara's abilities.

By this time I was doing some basic reporting for MCN on Brands' club races. I would compile a short report of about 100 words plus the results and call it through on a Sunday night. Bill liked this extra publicity, though it was always on the basis that if the sports pages didn't have enough space my little bit would be chopped first.

Bill gave me a season pass which was massively helpful. This would have been 1979 if I remember correctly. Names were being made and stars were rising. Racers like Keith Huewen and Gary Lingham. I think it was this season when Keith won 47 races in one year. He rode mainly in the 250 and 350 classes and was pretty much unstoppable. I got to know them both quite well and loads of others too. My contact list and phone book were getting bigger and bigger.

Sometime early on that season Bill Rose asked me to drop by his office, which I think was a porta cabin inside the paddock at Brands. Him and Barbara were there and as usual they were friendly and pleasant to me. In between barking orders at people and giving others a dressing down for not having the right paperwork, leathers or licence problems, they asked me if I would like to help the club out with an unpaid job of Bemsee PR and Advertising operative. I would just do what I was doing now but come to the monthly management meeting in the office at Dartnell Road, Croydon and hopefully generate some ideas and publicity for the club. I jumped at the chance. It was close to perfection. I would work at MCN during the week and go to Bemsee events at the weekends, which for the most part I was doing anyway, but have some sort of official status and purpose for being there.

And so it began.

I have already touched on the race I did at Chimay in Begium in summer 1980. It turned out to be a real moment in time and one which will be forever carved into my memory box. Just to cover off the basics Chimay is a charming little town in south west Belgium which is famous for two things; its Trappist Monks who brew a wonderful beer and the road circuit which is about 6km long including a 2km straight! The track has hosted car, bicycle and motorcycle races for many a year and attracted a good attendance from Britain in the last category. The event was incredibly well attended by thousands of fans, ran usually in late June or July so the weather was perfect and sat nicely in between Grands Prix so top flight riders like Barry Sheene, Michel Rougerie, Boot van Dulman etc could also fit it into their busy schedules. The event was called the Grand Prix des Frontieres.

Vic and I set off in the van with the outfit and all our kit to Chimay. Some hours later having crossed from Dover to Calais we arrived in this pretty little corner of Belgium. The paddock was set in a very large field which was literally a paddock inside the circuit which meant that we could leave everything there and walk into town back to our little B&B. Every class from sidecars to 500 Grand Prix bikes raced in their respective categories. Jaunty accordion folk music blared out just that little bit too loud all day from the Tannoy system all over town and in the paddock. Cheers could be heard from the crowds as famous riders took to the track for practice and qualifying. It was a very enjoyable race meeting held in good humour. A pleasure to be part of.

I would guess it was the Friday afternoon or Saturday morning I was wandering around the paddock and bumped into Barry. He was shocked to see me and asked what I was doing there. I told him about my passenger ride with Vic and his face dropped to gloom 'are you mad?' he said grabbing my shoulders.

On race day the sun was high and hot. We had done ok in practice but were still on the back row of the grid. I was feeling reasonably confident we could have a decent race. There was nothing to do for several hours so I strolled around the paddock and bumped into George Annuzet. I didn't know him to talk to but had heard his name and knew his face over the course of the week. He was the race director and chief of the events committee for the town of Chimay. I don't remember who but one of the English crowd introduced us so in my schoolboy French and his very broken English we chatted. It was clear he knew my name and had wanted to talk to me. He basically asked me if I would be interested in being the British rider representative for the following year. He needed someone to organise the entry and do all the paperwork and handle the rider payments. I didn't know there were rider payments! I said yes, well maybe, and with that he thrust his business card into my hand and asked me to contact him in a few weeks' time. I remember walking back to our van a bit shocked that George had heard of me and wanted me to help-out. Clearly someone had put my name forward but I never found out who. I have my suspicions though and Barry was fairly near the top of a short list. George had made it clear

25

that they handle Barry's agreement directly with him and I wouldn't be involved. If I understood him correctly he said I could have a budget of £3000 for all other British riders 'the same as we pay Barry!'.

Still in a bit of a daze and with pre-race nerves beginning to kick in a little I was then accosted by another rider, this time a German sidecar racer. He wanted to know if I was available to passenger him in the upcoming TT Races. He spoke very good English and told me how helpful it would be to have an English guy in the chair. There was absolutely no way I was interested or even able to ride the TT course so I politely turned him down.

What transpired over the next few hours was not only deeply disturbing but almost certainly unique. For sure I have never witnessed an event like it since, nor would I want to.

A bit of background info on the circuit is appropriate now. The Grand Prix des Frontieres is held on a road circuit of about six kilometres in length. It really is an open road for the rest of the year. Though basically a flat road circuit, towards the end of the lap and coming out onto the start finish straight is a wooded twisty section. Fast but slightly elevated leading downhill a little onto the grid area. The start finish straight is about four hundred metres long and ends with a ninety degree right hand corner taking the riders onto a longer straight flanked by the familiar open fields of the area.

After a quick sandwich lunch we were prepped for our race which, as usual, was the last of the afternoon so I had several hours to wait. I decided to watch the build up races from the pitlane area. This was no normal pit lane. For a start there were no garages or pit boxes. In fact the pit lane was a lay by running almost the full length of the straight and it backed right onto the very large field used as the paddock. The road fronting side of the pit lane was secured by a two level Armco barrier at which stood the mechanics etc holding out their rider's board. The rear of the pit lane, which was only one car's width or so had a single tier of Armco making it very low and easy to step over should the need arise. Entrance to the pitlane for spectators was via two or three gates in the paddock fence. I was placed about half way down the pit lane, the grandstands opposite though only perhaps twenty feet talk were packed with perhaps several thousand fans all cheering, waving flags and having a great time in the warm summer sunshine.

At the bottom of the pit lane was a caravan containing the clerk of the course, timekeepers etc. From where I was standing I could get a good look over the start area and then looking backwards I could see the riders charging away up the next stretch of the track after the right hander at the bottom of the start straight. Perfect, so I thought. What could possibly go wrong?

The heat rose, the atmosphere was building and the air was electrified with excitement. The music had been replaced by the commentators. If you love racing this event had everything including that unquantifiable thing of beauty, the sound of racing two stroke engines hanging in the air coupled with the smell of Castrol R. I was in heaven and loving every minute!

The 500 class race assembled on the grid taking the cheering to another level. Barry was front row and made a good push start (yes we were still in the era of push starts) and after that initial silence where you could only hear riders' feet on the tarmac as they pushed, the bikes burbled into life, then screamed away with a roar from the crowd.

Surprisingly I thought, there weren't many people in the pitlane area with me. Yes the Armco barrier standpoint was busy but only one person deep all the way down. Just along from me, about three people up was an enthusiastic photographer standing with one leg over the Armco. He was wearing a tee shirt, shorts and little Jesus boot type sandals.

The main group of riders went through on about lap two or three with a small gap behind them to the next bunch of riders. On the next lap immediately after the front runners came through, I heard a thump. A deep and hard thump followed by a screeching, scraping whooshing noise which was coming down the pit lane very very fast. In an instant a rider less bike spinning on its side shedding fairing parts and other bits and petrol spraying everywhere shot past me not two feet away. In fact it seemed to be attached to our Armco barrier. The noise was like a jet fighter taking off. Everyone was flung to the floor covered in bits and pieces and then another even heavier thump was heard as the bike hit the timekeepers' caravan at probably 80mph or even more.

Instantly I noticed two things as I looked up. Firstly the silence was so loud. No noise from bikes or crowd and a sort of suspended reality descended over the place. The other thing was the marshals were waving every red flag they could get their hands on.

Just a few seconds later I got to my feet and saw something horrific, a bare leg with just a Jesus type sandal was lying in the pit lane right in front of me. Still and clean cut below the knee. Bloodless and surrounded by nothing.

Then my eyes caught the photographer guy who was about eight feet from me flat on his back with his stump of a leg sticking up in the air pouring with blood. He started to howl and scream in a deep guttural, chilling way. It was a noise I cannot truly describe but will never forget.

People ran to him and tried to attend to him, though quite what they could do was very limited. The pitlane suddenly burst into life with people running everywhere. I stepped over the Armco taking my shirt off to cover the amputated leg only to be pushed back by a Policeman who appeared out of nowhere.

This was not the place to be any more, so I joined the race crews quickly getting back into the paddock and seconds later bumped into Barry who was running through the paddock. He was helmetless and very hot and bothered. 'Have you seen my dad?' he asked me and then ran off up to the top of the pit lane where he had last seen Franco.

I got back to our little team set-up to find Vic standing there. 'What the fuck just happened?' he shouted at me. I was shaking but told him as quickly as I could but blurted out the bit about the guy losing his leg. We all just sat down and listened to the mayhem which was still developing around us. Neither of us thought the races would continue but in just a few minutes or so it seemed the Tannoy announced that the race would be started again in half an hour or so. Surely not? But yes maybe a little more like an hour later the 500 race was re-started but like everyone else in the paddock they had lost interest.

Very quickly we heard what had happened. A local rider had lost control of his bike coming through the shaded twisty section before the start straight. He got into a huge tank slapper which threw him off but the bike stayed upright and clipped the top of the Armco at the pitlane entrance, sending it into a spinning torpedo in the pitlane where it clipped the heal of Franco Sheene dropping him to the ground. I heard a rumour later that afternoon that the rider was, amazingly, ok but that, sadly, the guy who lost his leg had died later in hospital. I must say that I cannot confirm that as it was just one of those rumours that quickly circulate after such an event.

Before I knew it, and still shaking, I was on the warm up lap and coming slowly onto the start line. I couldn't believe that we were going to race and to be honest my heart was not in it. We got a clean start and charged off chasing all the others. Vic got the farmhouse section wrong and nearly spat me out the front. In fact he did spit me out the front where I banged the track hard with my left hip. He had braked too hard when I wasn't expecting it. In an instant he reached forward and pulled me back into the outfit and we continued another half a lap before the engine gave way in a plume of white smoke. I was so relieved. A little later we were collected and deposited back in the paddock. The fans were filtering away, the buzz of the weekend was gone and everyone felt a bit deflated.

On the long drive back through Belgium, across to Dover and back up to London I decided that this wasn't for me. Sidecar passengering is hard and dangerous and I wasn't up to it. I could do it and at times really enjoyed it but life was getting busier all the time and if I was to take up George Annuzet's offer to organise the British rider contingent for the following year I would have even more on my plate.

It was now high summer 1980, The Bemsee season was in full swing and a new project was under way. Another one of my little ideas. We were to trial publish a Bemsee newspaper with me writing it all and trying to sell some ads to offset the costs. It was decided that a four-page A3 sheet would be sufficient for the first issue so I set about it. I had plenty of contacts in the print trade and of course knew many of the advertisers.

In reality it turned out easier and more successful than I had expected. At the next couple of Bemsee meets I interviewed riders, took pictures and generally made the best of what was on offer. We included results, rider features and gave a small slot to the calendar of forthcoming events.

The result was a smart, bright and interesting read that was sent to every member. I don't know if we made any money from it, possibly not but I do know it wasn't a total financial disaster.

The 1980 season came and went and If I remember rightly all in the Bemsee camp were happy campers.

Sometime over the late Autumn and into Winter 1980 at one of the monthly Bemsee management meetings Bill asked if I had any bright ideas for the club to generate more publicity for the coming season. He wanted something big, an idea that the national press and of course MCN couldn't ignore as a simple nothing event from the club racing scene.

As it happened I did have an idea, one which had been developing in my little head for some months. During the previous season, and certainly when I was chatting to everyone I could get in front of in the production of Bemsee News, a number of the racers I knew had complained that the season came along too soon before they had had a chance to test. The race season in those days was full of events and full of riders. Grids were often thirty or forty deep and the season started in early to mid-March so there was little time to get any meaningful track time in before the season kicked off.

My idea was crazy but I thought I'd run it past Bill and the team at one of the management meetings before Christmas 1980. The idea was simple Bemsee would put on a pre-season test day and open it up to every class of bikes, every rider in the club but with the added glamour, and certain publicity attraction of top British International and GP riders and teams.

I remember thinking that this idea would be shot down in flames due to any number of practical considerations. These would range from not enough time to organise it, no insurance, Brands Hatch not being available, weather concerns and risk.

Yet when I sat there at the large old table, much like a village hall, in the somewhat dark and dingy Bemsee main office looking at the faces of those gathered instead of laughter and throwing of hands in the air, they all smiled and said yes. The main face I looked at was of course Bill's. He was the boss and ran the place fairly but firmly. After my little speech he just shrugged his shoulders and said 'I like it. Can you do it?'

Of course I thought I could do it and so that evening we all pitched in with the various considerations and practical issues to be overcome and agreed a proposed date of 14th or 21st February 1981. Bill said Brands would be no issue whatsoever. A plan was agreed and I said I would contact all international riders I knew. Of course the big questions was whether we could get the main man to come. 'If we can get Barry to come we'll be guaranteed massive publicity but also fans will come too and most other top riders would want to be there and part of what could be an amazing celebration of British motorcycle racing.' Was Bill's summary.

I knew I could ask Barry and I felt he would not only listen to me but give it some serious consideration but though I knew his address I didn't have his telephone number. Even if I did I would be really scared and apprehensive to call him at home and ask him to come.

Over the next week or so things were put in place for the event, date was agreed and amazingly Brands were really helpful too. They said they would open up the main grandstand for free and Bill proposed that we only charge a £1 entrance fee because this wasn't about making money this was about publicity.

I wrote to Barry and Suzuki GB and quite a few other top riders to see if they would be interested. Bill and the team sent out an invitation to all Bemsee members and I also wrote and distributed a press announcement publicising the forthcoming unique event. Word spread fast. I would come home from work and find messages on my answerphone most of which were positive, but I hadn't heard from Barry. Without Barry's presence we would be swimming against the tide I felt.

Then one evening at home the phone rang, I answered it and heard the unmistakable voice of Barry. 'Ian it's Barry. Mate that's a great idea. I got your letter and having made sure I'll have the bikes and everything together, I'm in.' I was shaking and buzzing to hear from him. He was amazingly friendly and chatted about the event and what to do, how it would run and who we needed to get to ride. I had a list of riders I hadn't heard from and Barry amazingly offered to call them all. He said if he called them, they would say yes. So, we decided that he would call loads of people and I would call loads of people and between us we would er call loads of people! He then gave me his home telephone number which I was staggered at and said I could call him anytime. In addition saying he would contact people that week and call me back on Sunday lunchtime. I immediately remembered I was due to have Sunday lunch with my brother's new in-laws at their home so I told Barry. He wasn't fazed at all. He just said 'well give me that number and I'll call you there.'

We were motoring now. There was no way this wasn't going to happen

When I arrived at my brother's in-laws house I told Ray, my brother's father in law, that Barry Sheene might be calling me. He roared with laughter clearly not believing me. Ray was in the entertainment business putting on golfing and other sports events with a charitable aim where he would get comedians and famous actors to come along. But he didn't believe a word I was saying about Barry calling. You have to put this in context. Barry was a massive icon, a superstar, a household name, thus unlikely to be calling me at all let alone at someone else's house.

Sure enough sometime during the meal the telephone rang. Ray went to the hallway to answer it and came back with a shocked look on his face. Everyone at the table was quiet as he announced 'Ian it's for you, there's a bloke on the phone who says he's Barry Sheene.'

It was indeed Barry. He had been very busy calling other riders and gave me the list. He still had a few people to cajole and call but his final words that lunchtime were 'leave it to me

Ian, I'll make it happen'. There was no doubt we would now be certain of a bumper rider line-up and could announce names already to the media.

He was genuinely excited about the event and as a Bemsee old boy was glad to help out. We agreed to chat again later that week to tie up any lose ends. What did happen later than week was a rejection from Rex White, Team Manager of Suzuki based in Croydon. He wrote to me saying that they couldn't participate due to other obligations but wished us a great day and much success.

The intervening weeks were a mish mash of meetings, Christmas, New Year and detail planning as we drew ever closer to the event in February 1981. There was no programme as such and no special tickets for those hardy fans eager to see their heroes on the track for even a short time. Of course being a test event there would be no racing, no all day action but sporadic peaks as different classes and riders took to the track.

Now here's where it got interesting because suddenly there was a girl involved…

Please allow me a slight sideways step to introduce this part of the story because not only was it funny at the time but it came back to haunt me about 18 months later.

At the time I was still living at home with my parents in Bexley, Kent. In those days I was not folically challenged. I did, in fact, have a fine head of hair and my hairdresser was a mate called Vince whose showroom was in Bromley not far down the road from Boyer Kawasaki. They, Boyer, were also the home of the works Kawasaki GP team believe it or not.

Now Vince was a bit of a character. He had long flowing black hair and the charm of a charming thing in Charmland.

He had more crumpet on the go than any normal man could possibly want or deal with. His hairdressing salon was a fun place to be and once a month or so I would go in for a cut and blow dry. On recent occasions I had noticed a very attractive blonde girl doing the hair washing and at last she was there and washed my hair. You'll forgive me for not naming her. All will be clearer later.

She was just gorgeous. Model potential no doubt about it. Long blonde hair, a fabulous body and striking smile with great eyes and dressed sexily even when wearing a salon overall. We started chatting about this and that, the usual routine of 'have you booked your holidays yet?' and the like and found that we got on rather well. She was about my age, perhaps a little younger, but way out of my league. Then for some reason she started asking questions about me and what I like to do and where do I drink and the like. Before I knew it we had agreed to go for a drink. Yippee I was over the moon. She then went off for her lunch and Vince cut my hair grinning from ear to ear. He whispered in my ear 'she's a model you know. Only works here part time in between modelling work.' He then took a deep breath, stealing himself to tell me something important. 'You don't read The Sun then Ian? She's a Page 3 model!'

Me 'No'

Vince 'Yes she is my friend and here's the proof'

He quickly whipped out a copy of The Sun from a few days earlier and sure enough on page three was a wonderful vista of blonde honey bunch the girl who had just washed my hair. I could hardly stay seated.

Me 'But why would she want to go for a drink with me?'

Vince 'Because these girls look unavailable to most men and rarely get asked out you know.'

And a few days later we were in my car en-route to my favourite pub. None of my mates were expecting this woman of stunning looks to be on my arm that's for sure. When we walked into the pub, jaws dropped and beer was spilled. She looked like a million dollars. Over the weeks we went out lots of times and got along really well. She even showed me back copies of her appearances in The Sun!

The Brands test event was coming up fast and so I told her about it and asked if she wanted to come. Though she knew nothing about bikes or bike racing she had, of course, heard of Barry. She was really looking forward to meeting him.

In the final week before the Brands event the telephone was red hot. Bill Rose, Barbara and me were in constant contact checking and re-checking long to-do lists and must haves. Security, track staff, marshalls, catering, tickets, garage access, commentator and grandstand access. I must say in the run up and the event itself Brands Hatch management were amazingly helpful. They too saw this is a great way to start the season and good publicity for virtually no outlay or risk. The only problem on the horizon that week was the great British winter…

The weather for February was typical winter, cold! Snow flurries and rain and a cold wind. Not exactly ideal for a bike test day. But there was a glimmer of hope towards the weekend as the forecast suggested that things might thaw a little and even some milky sun might be arriving.

It became apparent in the ten days or so prior to the Brands test day that a considerable number of fans would be coming, rain, snow or sun. The Bemsee phones had been red hot with enquiries following an ad in MCN and some valuable editorial too. We had no idea how many would brave the weather but what we did know was the pitlane would be full. Every garage would be shared and full of bikes and riders.

On the morning of the event I leaped out of bed at the crack of dawn, literally, ripped the curtains back only to be faced with a scene of total devastation – snow! My house was barely 20 miles from Brands and so I was sure they had snow too. I showered, shoved some toast and tea down my throat and charged off in my little car. I collected Page 3 girl, let's call her Nina shall we, and we arrived there early, probably by 8.30am. There was snow the entire way there, though none had actually fallen en-route.

Having checked in with Bill and Barbara and with a look of failure on their faces we set off down through the famous Brands' tunnel in my car into the pitlane area. Already there were some guys active, fettling bikes and setting up garage kit. Barry had one of the first pitlane garages and his whole team with truck, caravan, cars etc were all there perfectly positioned at the back of the pitlane garages.

The snow was indeed lying on the track about an inch deep but it was not hard packed. It was one of those odd days in the winter where it didn't feel too cold even though it had snowed during the night. On-track testing wasn't due to start until I think about eleven so there was plenty of time for a sandwich and coffee and to meet and greet everyone.

The mood among the riders was really cheerful. People were excited about the day and even more excited to think that this was the only days away from the start of the season. By

10am bikes were revving in various garages and the pitlane was packed with riders and their families and mechanics. Nina was astonished and a bit out of place. She looked great but was probably a little bit over dressed for such an event. A bit glam.

I went into Barry's garage and shook hands with a few people here and there. His rear garage door was open, through which I could see he was standing by his caravan chatting to Steph and his dad. He then looked into the garage, saw me and Nina and wandered in.

To say this was surreal would be an understatement. He I was having organised this whole thing from scratch, with Bill and Barbara of course, and standing in the garage with Barry, my hero, with a beautiful page three girl.

Barry came up put his arms around me and gave me a hug. 'This is it then, you did it. It's just a great idea so let's get this thing moving and hopefully on the track later if that snow disappears'.

'I couldn't have done it with out you Barry, thanks for all your help'

'No problems Ian I was happy to get stuck in'

Though Barry was talking to me he was, for the most part looking at Nina. It turned out she had been on The Sun page 3 that very week and Barry sort of recognised her. I introduced them and they chatted for a short while during which time I realised Barry had the hots for her and yet over his shoulder I could see Steph not twenty-five feet behind him talking to others outside.

It crossed my mind that this could be very awkward very quickly if Steph saw him chatting up a girl. Luckily Nina needed the loo so she sloped off for a bit. Barry seized his chance and like a little schoolboy with a massive grin on his face asked all about her and how did I meet her and where does she live and if we were an item. The test day was totally forgotten by Barry for that minute or two.

By the time Nina returned we were back in the real world and Steph had joined us in the garage

The sound of two stroke engines filled the pitlane, the atmosphere was building. Barry had the good idea to walk out into the pitlane with Steph, me and Nina to see what was going on. What we didn't realise nor expect was a massive crowd of fans had now arrived and filled the Grandstand. Literally it was full with close to three thousand fans. As we walked out into the open a huge and very loud cheer went up. Barry was in his element. Hands waving and smiling ear to ear we went up to the pit wall and then walked along the garages shaking hands and chatting animatedly with various riders.

The weather had taken a slight turn for the better with the wintery blue and grey clouds lifting a little. There was even a hint of very weak sunshine but the snow hadn't shifted, though it had turned to a wet slush. The fans would be able to see everything as we were of course only using the Indy Circuit.

Barry made a decision and grabbed me as we walked back to his garage. A couple of 250 or 350 riders had gone out very gingerly a few minutes earlier and it appeared none had slipped off. We huddled in his cold garage to hatch a plan of attack.

'I'm going out Ian. If I go they all will. We need to get on track if only for some display laps. We owe it to the fans. I'll start spreading the word at this end of the pitlane, you walk along and tell everyone we going out in ten minutes.'

That was it. Time for action. I hurriedly walked along the pitlane spreading the word and as I left each garage door the previous garage occupants fired up their engines. Now all of a sudden instead of the odd bike being warmed up just for relief of boredom all engines were revving. The blue smoke coming out of the garages together with that amazing sound of two stroke racing engines ignited the fans who were now in a state of frost bite and high expectation.

In an instant we had action. Barry started out with, of course, full wet tyres followed by I think Dave Potter and Mick Grant but to be honest if you asked me now who was there that day I cannot remember. It seemed every British rider of any note was there but that would a slight exaggeration. The crowd roared and screamed as each rider very carefully entered Paddock Hill bend and then up the hill into Druids. One by one they filed out. No one fell off or slid into the mucky stuff. Barry did about six or seven laps and I think he went out later for another set as did many other riders but to be honest the job had been done.

The day drew to a close shortly after lunchtime. The light was fading fast and by about 3pm there was very little more to achieve. People on both sides of the track were still smiling. Some how we had pulled it off, yes everyone would have preferred much better and warmer weather but we all knew going into it that the weather might be against us. The attitude was what made this a success. I didn't hear one rider moan or refuse to go out.

I said my goodbyes to everyone I could and like many others drifted off into the now fading light of a February day. Oddly I never saw one photo from that day yet somehow today on Facebook groups it still comes up from time to time in people's memories. Bemsee had cemented its place as the Pre -eminent British motorcycle racing club and was shown to be leading the club racing feeder channel into the higher echelons of motorcycle racing, and that was what it was all about. Oh and it was a great day out.

Nina and I continued to see each other now and again for a few weeks but we drifted apart as her career took off. Little could have I known on that cold day at Brands Hatch that just four or five months later she would come back into my life from a very unexpected direction.

The buzz of that great day lasted far less than I had hoped. The real world kicks in pretty quickly with the back to work routine and it being very much a good memory but last week's news.

I was, however, very pleased and surprised to get a follow up telephone call from Barry some days later. He was really chirpy about the event and sure it would do the club and everyone involved some good.

1981. GPZ900 RACING, SNETTERTON AND SUZUKI GB

A lmost everyone of a certain vintage, the sort of vintage that would ensure you read a book like this, remembers the Yamaha RD350 one-make championship and the Pro-Am Challenge. To my recollection it was the first time anything like it had been organised in the UK and it was a stonking success.

But do you remember the Kawasaki GPZ900 one make championship just a year or two later?

The idea was that every Kawasaki dealer could get one of the bikes and sell it to or sponsor a rider of their choosing. I don't remember it being a massive success in terms of media coverage or track buzz but those who took part certainly knew they were in for a rough and bruising race series. It ran on the usual rules for this type of event; stock bike which could be altered by little or nothing apart from removing indicators etc. The problem was that the bike was heavy and didn't really handle that well.

A mate of mine at the time had managed to bag one of the bikes and with some local sponsorship was able to put together a reasonable package. He didn't win anything but like this type of racing it fostered a good paddock rivalry and camaraderie. Plus knee banging, elbow knocking on track action.

It was at one of these meets early in the 1981 race calendar at Snetterton where Suzuki GB came into my life most unexpectedly and changed it forever. I was wandering around the paddock at what was a seriously well supported event in terms of top teams and riders being present. Not sure what the event was but perhaps the first British Championship round of the season.

The Suzuki GB team were there right up at the top end of the pit garages. They had what seemed to me to be loads of staff, bikes, vans and tents etc and looked rather good. Ironically it was in that pit garage that I was based for the Motorcycle Mechanics 24 Hour test a couple of years prior.

Suzuki GB's managing director at the time was Denys Rohan. Not the tallest of guys but always with a boyish smile and a cigarette in hand and slightly rounded shoulders. Denys, who was in his thirties, had a full head of very black hair that was slightly slicked down, below which was a cheerful face in what my dad would have called swarthy skin. By that I mean he had a good tan. I had met him once or twice briefly but though I 'knew' him I didn't really know him and would not have expected him to approach me that day. Yet as I was drifting around the paddock, during a rest period in the programme at about lunchtime, I noticed Denys strolling towards me looking at me deliberately. It was one of those moments when you feel that the person is looking at you and then as they get closer and you're about to say 'hello' it turns out they are looking at the guy standing just behind you.

But Denys was actually looking at me though. He stood in front of me, we shook hands and he said something like 'Ian how are you? I'd like to talk with you later if you could come to the garage after the big race. I have something to talk to you about'. With that he smiled and walked back to the SGB garage. I was confused and excited. What on earth could he want to discuss? I had nothing going on with Suzuki and though I knew a few of their team loosely I just couldn't work out why he would want to meet me. Maybe I had upset someone or said something out of line somewhere. In any case I would find out later and so with a skip in my step and another glance up at the SGB garage crew area, I went off to enjoy the racing on this sunny afternoon.

An hour or three later after the racing was finished, or nearly so, I went up to the back of the SGB team pit garages. It was a busy place with bikes being loaded up and mechanics and riders packing things away. That year both Graeme Crosby and Randy Mamola were the main members of Texaco Team Heron Suzuki. The Heron part came from the Heron Corporation that was now the owner of the Suzuki GB empire. The Heron name was derived from the name of the company founder Henry Ronson, hence HERON. I knew the company was now run by the larger than life Gerald Ronson, son of the founder.

Denys was waiting for me and called me inside the garage.

He's always a pleasant man with a ready smile and a warm welcome. He beckoned me inside with a wave of his hand and we stood to one side with the semi chaos of team breakdown in full flow. The front garage doors were open inviting the passing officials and some fans who had managed to get into the pit lane to gawp and wonder at what life was like inside a real GP team. My mind was a bit fazed and buzzing all at the same time because looking at Denys I could tell he was itching to talk about something and it wasn't the weather.

He started with a little small talk about how long it would take the team to get back to Croydon and where did I live and the like then launched right into the meat and potatoes of what he had to say.

'You know Andy (Foulkes) has left us?'

Andy Foulkes being my ex MCN London office colleague who had been at Suzuki GB for a while but had apparently left abruptly very recently.

'Yes I had heard he was no longer there.'

'Well I'd like to talk to you about the job.'

I probably gave it away in my facial expression. An expression of surprise or even mild shock.

'I don't know really what the job is Denys.'

'It's Public Relations Manager for Suzuki GB.'

'But I don't know much about Public Relations Denys. Not at that level anyway'

'That's ok we'll tell you everything and I've heard good things about you Ian and know you can do it. Would you be interested?'

By now I was secretly shaking in my boots.

'Yes I would but I need to talk it all through with you because I'm not sure what you want.'

'Here's my card Ian call me tomorrow if you can and let's get you in to have a chat. I need to act fast on this, can you come in to see me at Beddington Lane this week?'

'Yes I think so.'

'Call me tomorrow and we'll arrange a date for this week.'

With that we both smiled, shook hands again and I left the garage wondering just what had happened. As I wandered back down to my mate's set-up in the back end of the paddock I was really confused. What had just happened, what was I doing with Denys Rohan's business card in my sweaty little hand. A card that said Managing Director Suzuki GB on it.

Like Denys said it takes an age to get back to Kent from Snetterton so on that drive down I was all at sea thinking about what happens next and very nervous too in case this was all a waste of time and a bit of a joke.

I needn't have worried that much because the very next day I called the main SGB number and asked to speak with Denys Rohan to find that I was put straight through to Deny's secretary who seemed to be expecting my call. She put me through to Denys. I was so excited I could have pissed my pants at that stage. Denys is a very calm individual; he has a deep voice that seems never to get too stressed or loud.

We had a chat about the weekend and how we got back from Snetterton and then into the detail of the call.

'Are you interested in what I had to say yesterday.'

'Yes very much Denys.'

'Can you come in to see us later this week because we need to act fast.'

'Yes Denys. Which day is best for you?'

We sorted out a date for either later that week or the Monday following and before I knew it I was driving into the small car park for the management offices and race team side of the business. I don't think I had ever been into SGB before but because I knew the area a little, I knew where it was and had no trouble finding it.

It's worth pointing out that Suzuki GB at that point was based in two different buildings in Beddington Lane separated by a plant hire company. So the main offices for cars, accounts, spares etc were fifty yards or so along the lane in several new or what looked to be new square typical two storey office buildings and warehouse accommodation. Most of the staff for all the divisions (bikes, cars, power products and marine) were based here.

The management offices were where I was going to see Denys and based in a large Victorian double fronted house with a central main door, room for perhaps ten cars at the front. Today the car park had a few Jaguars and a Rolls Royce. I cannot remember what car I was driving but I felt decidedly out of place parking my excuse for a car alongside these executive carriages.

They seemed to be expecting me, Denys' secretary met me and took me into her small office which in turn led into Denys' office, which was surprisingly small and at the back of the main office on the left of the ground floor. Denys met me with a big smile and a warm handshake just like at Snetterton.

What happened next was a bit of a blur as he mapped out what the job entailed and what I would be paid and then before I knew it he told me he wanted to offer me the job but needed me to meet the Group Managing Director John Turner. At which point he knocked on a connecting door from his office which opened and I was led straight into the main ground floor front office which was huge. Sitting at the desk in the bay window was John Turner. Now John was a bit of an enigma to me. He was slim, tall, well dressed, had a proper hand shake and a full head of sandy hair that was slightly tinged with silvery white. He was also friendly and welcoming. We all sat down and very quickly they summarised the job, my strengths and being the ideal fit for it and asked me if I wanted it. It was clear they were anxious to get this post filled and that they hadn't advertised it and wouldn't be if I accepted.

How on earth could I say no?

I don't think I was there an hour. I never saw a written job description mainly because they were almost unheard of in those days and I also knew I hadn't asked any detailed or decent questions. The next thing I knew they were summing it all up checking my home address to which they would send a written job offer and asking when I could start.

Smiles all round and I was out the door. I didn't even get to see around the place and meet a few people. I had no idea where my office would be and how the job would unfold or what to expect.

A day or so later the job offer arrived which turned out to be better than I had expected. I think the pay was a little more than they had told me, the job came with a new company car to be decided and a full expense account with a Texaco fuel card. All I had to do was accept and agree a start date.

To be honest the next week or so before I started was a total mess with me having serious doubts about taking it on mainly because I was still uncertain what 'it' was to be. I had plenty of low level PR experience, was a good advertising man and was well connected in the bike world as I knew it but this was an elevation way beyond my comfort zone. But I was committed to it and very excited by the thought of a) working at Suzuki GB and b) working on motorcycle marketing and PR all day every day.

The first day arrived far too quickly for my liking and with huge nerves and a sense of stepping into the unknown I arrived at Suzuki GB Beddington Lane to start work as Public Relations Manager. Wow I was so excited!

I reported at the main offices along the lane and instead of being taken into a large open plan office with most of the other staff like I expected was told to go immediately to the management office where I had met Denys and John a week or so before. Arriving here I was met once more by Denys' secretary and John Turner's secretary Gill. They both seemed quite excited that I was there and ready to get stuck in. I was told to follow them to my office and to my shock and horror they went up the main staircase in the management house/ building turning swiftly right at the top and up another couple of steps into what was a small office to the side of the building. Waiting for me with a huge smile on her very pretty face was Sue, my secretary. She sort of gushed with a sense of relief which I soon realised was because replacing Andy Foulkes was well overdue and somewhat of a difficult task. The other two ladies left me with Sue but they all agreed that very soon I needed to be walked around the whole place so I could get my bearings and know where everyone was and where all the departments were located. This was my first warning of what would turn out to be a massive miscalculation on my part.

This was because they said they would introduce me to all the key staff members of each department like Marine, Cars, Parts, Racing etc.

I sat at my desk and almost the first thing Sue said was that the phones ring all day and that I needed to write a press release announcing my arrival and send it out by fax that day to all the bike papers and media. She said that in between the phone ringing almost as soon as she put it down. It was chaotic in the media office as I used to think of it.

What was clear and very frightening to me was that I still didn't know what my job entailed but was beginning to get an understanding that it didn't stop at Suzuki Motorcycles which is what I thought it was.

After what seemed like a short time only the girls from downstairs came back up so that all four of us could go for a wander. Both Denys and John Turner were off site that day and that gave a welcome breathing space, Denys did call me from his other meeting soon after I had touched down and welcome me to the mad house and immediately asked if I was going to the race meeting that weekend at Donington Park, if I remember correctly. He quickly followed up when I failed to give him an immediate answer that my job included all race team PR and media management and that usually he and other directors do not go to many race meetings and so they would expect me to go. Furthermore, that only Rex White, the team manager, and me would be the regular 'managers' at race meetings.

I assured him I would be there but inside realising I had no idea what I was going to be doing, where I would stay, had no passes or any understanding of what my role at a race event for SGB would actually be.

What I learned in a day or two was things moved fast at SGB, very fast. If you said you would do something not only was it then expected that you would do it professionally but that any help or advice you needed would be forthcoming very quickly.

Our first stop in the first day new boy tour was the main management building in which I was based. Upstairs in the main body of the house were the senior executive offices for Peter Agg- Chairman, Maurice Knight- Sales and Marketing Director and Edna Calder- main board director and what I soon perceived as second in command to Peter Agg. These people were formidable and not to be under-estimated on any level on any day. I'll come back to these people and the company set-up shortly because I think it's well worth some of your time.

Our next step on the tour was the race team workshop and general bike workshop behind our building. There was a driveway to the left hand side of the building which was tight but could accommodate race trucks and vans etc but there was the way into these workshops from a rear door out of the building. They were connected to the main building and so we walked through from the building into the workshop area to meet and greet everyone. To a man and woman they all seemed genuinely happy to meet me and eager to get a bit of time with me to explain things that I would be involved in.

At last I was taken through to the race workshop which was everything I hadn't expected. My vision was that of a pristine well-lit area with work-stations, top end tools and equipment and a hushed sense of purpose.

What I found was a shock. It was like any other workshop, if a little bigger, filled with parts and bikes and benches and oil and a light-hearted buzz about the place. There was an office which was much cleaner and brighter but that's because it was where Linda Ratcliffe worked. Linda was I suppose team co-ordinator or administrator but I was to realise she was the glue that held it all together. She booked all transport, hotels, tickets, admin, liaised with suppliers, airlines, channel ferries, circuit owners and so on. In short if she didn't do it Suzuki GB didn't go racing. It's also worth noting that Suzuki GB ran two complete race teams. First and foremost was the works Suzuki grand prix team direct with and for the factory. This had always been the case since the late sixties or early seventies. Then there was the Suzuki GB race team which contested all the other international events and home championships. Linda was super friendly to me and asked if she could come up to see me after lunch to brief me on things. My heart rate surged because it was becoming clear to me by the minute that my role did indeed include the race team but also that any involvement I still had with Bemsee would have to stop immediately. There would be no time for both.

It was at that moment that I met, the now late but very great, Rex White, team manager of Suzuki. Now it's hard to do justice to just what a lovely man Rex was. He was by then in his fifties I would say, with a cherubic face and white hair and an obvious limp. A bit on the heavy side and holding on to a lifetime of sporting experience. He was softly spoken always calm and very pleased to see me. I was beginning think that there must be some sort of secret briefing note on me or that they were told to be uber friendly to the new boy in case he left for some reason. Rex welcomed me to the team and was sure we would get along fine. He had also been spoken to by Denys already because he said how he knew I would be at Donington that weekend and looked forward to it. 'I understand your background and history in racing. You did the pre-season test day at Brands which we all know was a great day so it'll be good to work with you'. He excused himself as he had to press on and so did we.

The next stop on the tour was the other side of the business along the lane. There were two people to meet who were important for me to know. Firstly Eric Allvey who was Parts Director and a very important man. His job was to ensure all parts for all products were ordered, in stock, flowing out to dealers and priced correctly. Parts is an often-overlooked section of the business but in fact can generate more revenue and profit than the complete machines themselves. What I noticed most about Eric, apart from that is, the once again very friendly welcome he gave me (it was beginning to feel like The Witches of Eastwick) was his secretary Lynn. She was right up my street and very attractive. More later...

The most important man on this side of the business was the managing director of the car division, John Norman. I knew of John before because he used to run Kawasaki Motors in UK. Not sure I had ever met him but I was eager to this time. He was altogether more business like and less friendly. But he was approachable in a big boss kind of way. He immediately struck me as a man with little sense of humour and a man with a mission in life. As it turned out over the years I got to know him much better and for some reason he seemed to want to take care of my career. Most of that happened after I left Suzuki, and for reasons never explained to me, John would keep in touch and twice engineered possible jobs for me. Sadly John died at a young age in the mid noughties.

If I look back at those days in Beddington Lane I cannot remember what we did for lunch. There was no works canteen or similar and Beddington lane was a bit of a waste land so we must have sent out for sandwiches but it hardly mattered because the pace of work was fast and furious so any free time at lunchtime time was soon used up by treading water.

Just as Linda from the race team had promised she arrived in the office soon after lunch with a box of stuff for me. She was bright, sharp minded and quick to organise and sort out kind of girl. She got things done and that's what I soon understood at SGB, you had to cover ground every day and get things done.

In her box for me were tickets and a car pass for the Donington weekend ahead. A team box of un-named, in other words non personalised, clothing. I think there was a team jacket, white team shirt, team sweat shirt and a hat or two. She assured me my personalised team wear would arrive inside week or two. By that she meant that I would have my name embossed or stitched onto my team long sleeved jacket and body warmer. She also gave me the details of the team hotel for Donington and asked what time I would be arriving on Friday. I had no answer because it was my first day so I turned to Sue my already trusty secretary who said that the best thing to do would be to leave here about twelve so I could be at the track by about 4pm.

That seemed to make sense to me and that's when our super spares plan was agreed upon. I think the race team had been hoping for this for a long time but I'm not sure Andy used to attend race meetings much. He was much more into off road events which were not part of the SGB area of responsibility, given that oddly SGB were not the importers of Suzuki MX and enduro bikes, this was left to Graham Beamish at Portslade in West Sussex.

The Super Spares Plan had been hatched by Rex and Linda and was to be agreed by me and put into immediate action. Remember this was pre mobile phones and of course pre internet so communications were slow and low tech. Telephone boxes and fax machines were considered state of the art in them days!

For any race meeting the race team would plan a list of parts and spares they might need for the weekend ahead. The vans and trucks would be loaded up usually on a Tuesday each week and added to as the day progressed and then late on Wednesday or perhaps Thursday they would head off. Now if they were racing at Brands Hatch there was no issue to worry about but if they were at Mallory, Silverstone, Donington etc they inevitably had issues with any late parts they might need. That is where I would come in. It had been agreed that I would attend all UK race events and those special one offs such as the North West 200 and the Ulster GP plus a few grands Prix such as France and the Dutch TT.

In each case but mainly for the main UK season I would leave the office on a Friday lunchtime, sometime during the morning Linda would pop into the office to collect my car keys. She would have had a phone call or fax with the list of items required which she would then load into my car leaving enough space for me and my stuff. Then she would return the car keys and with a smile breeze off back to her office.

And that's how it worked out. A perfect plan. I never knew what would be stowed in my car and often found that the things I had to take to the circuit were very unusual. Fairings and the odd wheel were normal but there would be boxes of pistons, gear change and hand levers, seat assemblies, even gearboxes and heavier stuff. I also had to take team give-aways like Tee Shirts and boxes of stickers. Always stickers, we seemed to get through thousands every weekend. So when I would arrive at the circuit my first and only job on that Friday was to get as close to the team garage as possible and get some help offloading everything. This was never a problem as they were always pretty eager to get their hands on my little stash of spares.

All this was organised on my first day!

In the first few days of my first week if I remember correctly, I met so many people and bonded firmly with Sue my sec. She was an amazing lady who smoked like a trooper but got so much work done. She also knew the full extent of my job but was savvy enough to ease me in over those crazy early days in week one.

For example, she knew that my job was absolutely definitely not just for the motorcycle division but as a marketing support service for all divisions. When I realised that I was in even more shock. Not only was I employed five days a week in the full time job as PR man for the SGB bike division and weekend race media man but was also supposed to serve cars, marine, power products and corporate too!

But there was more. My responsibilities also included running the press motorcycle fleet. In other words managing the ins and outs and egos of the press when they wanted a test bike for a day or week. That meant fielding requests, getting the right press on the right bike in the right order of importance and publishing date, especially when launching a new bike. MCN were always top of the list. But it also meant coercing press into testing bikes they definitely didn't want but I needed some coverage of. So inevitably some horse trading was engaged in. 'I'll give you this if you test this for me now'.

Back to my first weekend with the race team which was a baptism of fire without flames etc. My car had been loaded up by Linda and so I set off into the Friday afternoon traffic to do battle up to Donington. I say Donington but to be honest I really don't remember what my first race was with Suzuki. I'm fairly sure it was Donington though so we'll go with it.

I got to the track gained easy access with my passes, got parked up close enough and found myself in the busy but empty paddock. Donington paddock was huge and though it was packed with vans and trucks there was hardly anyone around. Unlike race weekends when the tracks were full and the paddock was a target for hundreds of people trying to gain illegal access, on Fridays it seemed so calm and empty.

Rex saw me coming and smiled a smile of relief. They needed some of the spares to repair a bike that had been down the track. My car was emptied by a couple of the boys and after I had familiarised myself with the team layout etc I wandered into the media office upstairs had a chat with a few people, introduced myself to a few others and enjoyed a really good relaxed afternoon at the track.

Not sure if it was this event or one shortly afterwards but I bumped into Barry. He knew I was now at Suzuki and stopped to ask me lots of questions about the place. If such and such was still there and what did I think of so and so? He was pleased that I was in the job but strangely over the next couple of years though we saw a lot of each other we didn't really talk much save for a hello and how are you doing type of chat. Things were a bit different at Chimay in June '81. More later.

In week two at SGB I already felt my feet were under the table. Things moved fast as I have said and there was no time to sit back and wait to be bedded in. It was clear to me already that the way of doing things at SGB was to grab your job and make things happen. You made your job your own and if that meant taking things by the horns and steering it one way or another, that was just fine. It was a grown-up professional work ethic. You were accepted into the family very quickly and just got on with things. There was no micro-management, you were expected to know your stuff and deal with the right people to move things along. Though I reported to each divisional head my main boss was of course Denys with whom I got on very well. He was a busy guy and though we saw each occasionally during the week but not as much as I had expected to.

Visitors seemed to be the one staple during the week. Especially in my first few weeks which were rushing by at a rate of knots I had never experienced before I joined. In those early days Keith Huewen, Graeme Crosby, Big Mick (Graeme's chief mechanic) and of course Dave Radar Cullen, also one of Croz's mechanics. Radar was always drifting into the office not to see me of course but to see Sue, who he was totally besotted with.

Keith and I had known each other for a couple of years already as he was a very successful club and national rider so it was at the Bemsee events we got to know each other. He was now sponsored by **sdc building**, a local company to him where he lived and was essentially a British Championship rider retained by Suzuki GB. He was a regular at Beddington Lane to catch up with the management and to schmooze the right people.

It was in the first week I would guess that The Bag arrived on my desk. It was a black nylon zip up bag about a foot square. Sue brought it to me and said 'you'll need this everywhere you go, it's the camera bag'.

I was not a very good photographer and so was very confused by all this equipment in the bag. Two or three Nikons, motor drives, flash units, lenses etc. To be honest I didn't know much about frame speed and different lenses so I got a book from WH Smith which I think was called Photography For Wallies and quickly read up on it. The idea being was that though we used professional photographers for product shots and official events we didn't have anyone else for the day to day team shots and product shots that might be needed for press releases. That was my job. So I just got stuck in and learned a little about taking pictures. Another responsibility that I never knew I needed.

Tom Waterer was another who dropped by on a regular basis. Tom was motorcycle national sales manager and as such was out on the road most of his week but being a detail man and also liking to be well connected he would drop by for a chat and to see if I knew anything new about anything about to happen. I liked Tom and could see his dedication to the brand and the company.

Talking of the company I think it is worth explaining how Suzuki GB was made up and who was leading it forward.

Peter J Agg was an inspirational character and at the top of the tree, so to speak, of the day to day executive directors. He was Chairman of the company and it was he who had started Suzuki GB back I believe in 1969 when the incumbent Suzuki distributor went bust. There must be an amazing story about how that company managed to screw it up but I have never got to the bottom of it all. Peter Agg who was always referred to as PJ was the wealthy self-made businessman distributor of Lambretta scooters for the UK. He had made a ton of money doing this during the boom period for scooters but that was on the wane, thus he was the perfect candidate to take over the reins of Suzuki motorcycles for the UK.

PJ's second in command and long time collaborator was Maurice Knight. Maurice had been sales manager with PJ on the Lambretta success and together they formed SGB with Peter putting in the money alongside I think some investment from a bank. Maurice soon became sales director and then sales and marketing director of SGB.

It's worth also knowing how they complemented each other because they were like chalk and cheese in my opinion.

PJ was a tall and grand stature of a man. He always wore immaculate probably hand made suits and together with his swept back thinning grey hair, and handlebar moustache he would dominate any room he entered. He had an impressive air about him which was helped not a little by his upper class and clipped but very enjoyable to hear plummy accent. He was a passionate man and loved the finer things in life. Never far from his lips was a large cigar, never far from his hands was the steering wheel of any number of cars like Rollers, Porsches and the like. He lived and breathed hard work and success. But he also had a temper and when he exploded people would dive for cover or run for the nearest door!

My office was separated from his by I think one small corridor and one wall so when he was bollocking someone or letting rip about an issue he was far from happy with he could be heard loud and clear. He also had one of those thumper veins in his forehead, which was pumped up by pressure and blood, would literally be visible from twenty five feet away. Time to keep well clear. He was a leader, hero to many in the company and a trailblazer. I loved him and kept in contact over the years after I left SGB. He was always kind and answered my emails. I had started writing a book about the history of SGB with him when he most sadly died in about 2012/13. This book has partly been inspired by him and the book we never wrote.

Maurice Knight on the other hand was more of a car salesman but that is perhaps a bit unkind. He was as sharp as a tack, knew exactly how to present a product or sales idea. Knew the British bike market inside out together with probably everyone in it and was also passionate about winning and bike racing.

He seemed to me to have arms and legs that might be connected to a third body as they never seemed to be in sync with the rest of his own body. His suits were just a little on the large size and his sense of humour and cutting tongue were the stuff of legend too. He was one of those directors or leader where when you were invited into his very large office across the way from mine you were initially delighted and flattered to have made it into that sales meeting, but then you hoped he never ever called on you to answer a question or make a serious comment. Mainly because he would rip people to shreds if they didn't know their stuff. But he seemed to me to be a fair man and together with his razor-sharp sense of humour was great company. Like PJ I had kept in touch with Maurice over the years seeing him at industry events long after he retired. He was always pleased to see me and never forgot my name or events and funnies from my time at SGB. At the time of writing I believe Maurice is alive and well.

Next in line you had John Turner who was group managing director and a Heron man. Heron via Gerald Ronson had bought the majority shares in Suzuki GB in about 1975 as the company had grown rapidly and very successfully. This meant the cash required and business infrastructure would benefit from a larger corporation. Ronson owned the Heron motor group which included petrol stations and some up-market car dealers so it sort of fitted.

I must say that Gerald Ronson was never seen by me at any time on the premises of SGB except for the opening day of Suzuki GB's new headquarters in Crawley more of which later in this book.

Below John Turner were the divisional directors of cars =John Norman, bikes Denys Rohan (another Heron man) and sundry other directors such as Eric Allvey = parts.

But there was another key person on the board who was as impressive as both PJ and Maurice combined. Edna Calder.

Edna was a long time associate of PJ, strictly business as far as I could see. She was a wonderful lady who I got on well with though always at a distance particularly in my early days. She was a bit like the Queen. She knew her brief, watched everything, knew what people did and more importantly did not do and could cut you in half with a single sentence. What is sometimes referred to as a withering reducer. She sat on the main board and it seemed to me acted as a guide and hand brake to PJ when he got carried away or needed a valuable second opinion.

PJ and Edna it appeared to me had a selection of other businesses together mainly in the hospitality sector. They owned Brantridge Park in Sussex, a very upmarket boutique hotel. The Bridge House hotel at the top of Reigate Hill next to the M25 and a place I used quite regularly over the years, and no doubt other businesses I was unaware of too. In fact in 1982 PJ opened his new hotel on his own estate called Effingham Park. Though it wasn't strictly my area I was asked by him to do some PR and marketing work on the side for the opening which I was very happy to do.

I think at this point I should mention two other players or characters who were involved with SGB and who troubled me somewhat in those early days. I had nothing to be worried about, but my initial impressions were concern and discomfort.

The first was Charles Agg, PJ's son and heir. Charles was about my age and had that air of public school boy about him. He was always looking at things on my desk. He was perfectly friendly and seemed to care about how I was settling in, but I worried that actually he wanted a role like mine. It would suit him down to the ground if his ambition was to take over a more senior role in the business at a later date. He was a good looking bastard too with bleached blond crimped hair. I kept my mouth shut but asked Sue is he was ok. He would wander in have a chat about nothing much, smile a lot and then disappear. The fact of the matter was that he didn't work in the business, had no intention to, never interfered in what I was doing and was actually a really nice bloke. There was a time when I was flying in an out of Gatwick Airport a lot and it seemed I would bump into Charlie every time.

The second player was David Farquhar, pronounced Farker. He was the corporate public relations man for the company and the car division. He ran his own public relations concern from his very substantial house in West Sussex and was connected to the company directly to PJ so that was worrying too. He spoke with a very affected and slightly effete plummy accent, always dressed like he was about to go to Royal Ascot and no doubt was a world champion gin and tonic abuser. He would often come into my office and always with a cigarette on the go, smiling constantly and drag me off to the pub for a quick lunch and 'catch up'. The first few times I met David I was very put off by him. I couldn't work out if he hated me and hated the way Andy wasn't around anymore. Or if he liked me and was happy Andy wasn't around anymore. He also had this very upper class way of referring to everyone by their second name. Thus he would say Foulkes instead of Andy. He once referred to me as Burgess in the car park at the office when we came back from the pub and bumped into PJ. PJ started it off by talking to David about me when I was standing right there with them! PJ asked Farquhar 'how's Burgess getting on then?'. I didn't know what to do, should I stand there and let them talk about me as if I wasn't present or butt in and excuse myself?

David's response to PJ was 'he's doing more than fine and is getting along with everyone'.

All very strange I thought but just like Charles Agg. David turned out to be a gem of a guy who was never less than helpful and supportive even though he could see that maybe I would do some of the PR work in-house that he might have otherwise done.

Some years later after leaving SGB I was having lunch with a client at The Bridge House in their busy and very excellent lunch dining room. I hadn't seen Edna sitting in the corner of the room having lunch with a guest when the waiter arrived at my table with a bottle of wine which I hadn't ordered and a message. 'Mrs Calder sends her regards and best wishes and this bottle for you to enjoy'. I was genuinely shocked and turning around saw her smiling face from the corner table. She waved at me and mouthed 'enjoy'. After our lunch I drifted past her table gave her a hug and thanked her very much for the wine. She was a class act.

Another oddity about the daily life of Suzuki GB was the memo system. Never seen it since or before, it was unique. Remember this was before emails and mobile phones. SGB had this internal post system which was driven it seemed by the need to cover one's arse with the help of the pink memo system. The idea was that when one had agreed to do something or had got another manager or staff member to agree to do something one would quickly follow up with a little memo reminder. The form was pink and it was about A5 sized. You could send it same day and copy whoever you liked on it to prove that a job was actioned or someone else had agreed to take it on. The first thing I learned about this system was to see who had been CC'd on it. The directors initials in the CC box were crucial. Thus if you got a memo from say Tom Waterer which had been CC'd to DR, MK or worse still PJA then the idea was to drop everything and get the work done or at least started because others would follow it up or it could and probably would be used against you at a later date. If you got a memo from a director you just did it immediately anyway but always writing back with another pink memo to announce it was done and thus collect Brownie points for free. If you ever got a memo from one of the SGB directors and saw the initials GMR on the top you just shit your pants, went into warp speed and got it done because GMR was Gerald Ronson.

What nobody seemed to know was that my cousin Graham Saunders as mentioned earlier in the book was a Suzuki employee too or at least had been. I thought he had left SGB by the time I arrived but one day in my second week I walked slap bang into him in the back yard to the other building. We both just stood there looking at each other in amazement. Graham's little cheeky Oliver type grin on his face he said 'I was wondering when I'd bump into you. I knew you were here because I saw the memo'. I told him I didn't know he was still here and asked him why he hadn't been over to say hello. He just said 'well I didn't want to bother you'. Graham always understated. He was, it turned out in charge of the training centre for the bike division. He ran all the technical tests, dealer mechanics training sessions and anything oily and dirty that the race team couldn't get involved with or didn't want to get involved with. He also did what he called 'special projects' which included things like taking hated existing bikes and engineering mods and possible changes to go back to the factory to implement so the bike could be saved from the scrap heap.

As it happened Graham did indeed leave SGB a few weeks later to set up on his own as a two stroke tuner and motocross engineer.

So what exactly was my job and how did it run my life?

Having now been in situ for some weeks the job spec and profile were well developed. During the week I was PR man to the company and on hand to help anyone in any product group who needed something that their ad agency, if they had one, didn't do for them. Public Relations was only the start of what I was asked to do. Really it was a full service marketing services office that Sue and I ran. My feet rarely touched the floor, no two days were ever alike and I completely loved it. For example I mentioned a while back that Suzuki GB were not the importers of Suzuki motocross machines etc. That's true because it was all done by a completely separate company owned and run by the late and very great Graham Beamish. So I was surprised one day to be called in to Denys's office and asked to attend a meeting at Beamish headquarters in Portslade that afternoon. I must have asked Denys why we were involved etc but it seemed they needed some help with a bit of marketing and my name came up. So at lunchtime I set off down the Purley Way A23 towards Brighton and the pleasures of the coast for a sunny afternoon. My pleasure was soon interrupted by a bang and a flat tyre. In my smart shirt and light grey trousers I was mucking about by the side of the road changing a wheel before getting on with my journey hot, bothered and covered in grease. When I got there somewhat late the meeting was in full flow. I had never met Graham Beamish before and was embarrassed that on my first visit I was such a shambles. I washed up as best I could and sat down.

In fact Graham was a delight. He was fine about my late arrival and began to gently take the piss out of me all the way through. I now knew where Andy Foulkes got his 'off road' sense of humour from as I knew he and Graham were pretty close.

I'm not sure if it was at that meeting or another a week or so later but he asked me back to see the other part of his operation based at Golding Barn Farm which he owned a few miles away. Graham was a delight to be with and we got along very well from the off. I still hadn't worked out that SGB were about to acquire his business and roll the off-road operation into the main business within a year.

We stood outside his house on the very long patio and chewed the cud for a while. The view of the rolling Sussex Downs and beautiful countryside was stunning. He told me he had the farm and so casually I asked him how much land he had. Graham paused for a moment then rocked around on his toes easing from side to side to get a good view before saying 'well as we stand here everything you can see, is mine'. Jesus Christ from where I stood he seemed to own most of Sussex. He then informed me the total land he owned was about eleven hundred acres!

So aside from these little interludes which were always good fun and unexpected my day job was PR man which involved a lot of writing of press releases, product briefings, press meets, running the press motorcycle fleet, attending all manner of marketing and or sales meetings for the product groups, planning product launches and events. Plus the dealer meetings in hotels and at SGB from month to month. One of the biggest benefits to me was that I was allowed to ride and borrow any bike I liked from the press fleet. Heaven, or so I thought. I would stroll around the workshop and gaze lovingly at all these bikes that I could simply book out whenever I liked. The problem was they were often out on loan and I never had any spare time to ride them. Weekends were almost always taken up with racing and if not I was in bed trying to sleep and chill out, or the weather was rubbish and I didn't want to ride these beauties in bad weather. The only real time I got to ride a bike was by leaving my car at work and taking one home at night to ride it back in the morning. Not much fun but that was how I got my leg over a good few of the bikes.

My weekend job was racing team media manager. In a way I was a different person at the race tracks. As I have mentioned earlier I was spares mule for the team arriving Friday mid afternoon for most events and then as things got more interesting on Saturday and Sunday I revved it up and fulfilled my media role which was a mix of meeting race reporters from the nationals and specialist press plus of course there was usually a representative of local radio and television. My job was to get stories of Suzuki into their hands so I would shake a few hands wander around and chat to them, linger in the press box a little. Try to get the riders interviewed and some other coverage if we could think of something.

The there was the corporate side of things which meant meeting sponsors past and present and perhaps even future, giving out little gifts to selected people and even getting a fan into the garage for a ten minute exposure session. I was the face of Suzuki Racing so I had to be available. My role was not to get in the way of Rex and the team and definitely was not a racing role at all. I also had to keep unwanted people or media away from the team and that sometimes could cause friction.

I was never less than surprised that Maurice Knight and Denys Rohan or indeed any other SGB director almost never came to a race meeting. I suppose it was because I met Denys at Snetterton that I thought they would always be in attendance but that was not the case at all. For the most part it was Rex White as Team Manager and me as Media Boy representing the company. Rex was very much senior to me in the company and so I would sometimes try to defer to him. It didn't really work that way though because he did the race stuff and I did the rest. I never trod on his toes and he never ever told me what to do though being the star that he was he was always available to discuss something or run an idea by at the team hotel in the evenings. We worked well together which would stand us good stead for the events that would unfold at the North West 200 in May 1982...

Life was good and busy. Racing was successful and good and busy. Part of my job was to write a very short race review and attach the results for staff consumption first thing on a Monday morning. The directors got a copy hand delivered to their desks and the staff notice boards were next on my list.

In a way I never really felt I was part of the race team because I wasn't actually involved in the on-track part of it. But in other ways I was totally submerged in it. All the team from riders and mechanics to Rex at the top were very friendly and accepted me totally as part of it. Personally I loved it. What was there not to love? I was in the pits of the team as part of the team organising media coverage and team exposure to the fans and sponsors and I had all the badges I needed plus a room and food paid for. Usually I was given a single room which was fine but on occasion I would have to share a twin room with a mechanic which was also fine because it was more fun. But it was work and so we had to behave. No late night drinking, no lateness, always fresh team gear on show and generally keep it quiet. Race teams are in my opinion no place for loud mouths.

The riders mixed in with everyone. There was absolutely no 'us and them'. We were all one unit and it worked. Quite often we were using the same hotel as the other main teams so we would casually mix but keep our distance from Honda and Yamaha but we all knew each other. Barry seemed to always have a different hotel for him and his team. I don't think I ever saw Barry in the same hotel as us.

In late June after another and busy week Denys called me into his office. When I got there he had a grin on his face which I now knew showed that he was planning something. He sat me down and told me that the following weekend we would clear off to the Dutch TT. I wasn't planning to go but he decided we could share the driving in his Jaguar and have good weekend away with the team at what was one of the best race venues God has ever given us.

We left late on the Thursday if I remember correct, drove to Dover got the boat to Calais and a few hours later arrived at the team hotel. Got to our rooms and crashed out.

Race day at the Dutch TT is for some reason always on the Saturday. So Friday morning after an early breakfast Denys told me that he had a pass for the circuit but I didn't! Not to worry he said, his secretary had organised my pass to be collected at the media centre which was in the middle of town. He gave me the keys to his car and we both drove to the media centre where he hitched a lift with one of the team cars and left me there. Thanks Denys. I think the building used was a local authority library or office and had a long internal corridor down to a central hall where queues of people were waiting to register. In fact it didn't take long to get my accreditation and I was back out into the car park which was now much more empty.

I jumped into the car and tried to start it. It wouldn't. I kept tuning it over but it just wouldn't fire up. This was a car I knew nothing about, hadn't ever driven before an hour ago and the owner, Denys had disappeared. I got out to take a look under the bonnet and heard some giggling coming from the bushes at the end of the car park about twenty feet away. Under the bonnet I found the issue and heard even more laughter coming from the bushes. Who knew bushes could laugh, but these were. Some lunatic from a certain Grand Prix team had decided to change all the HT leads around so it wouldn't start. Car doors slammed, giggling stopped and the culprits sped off to the circuit. I was left to work out the bundle of spaghetti under the bonnet and get the bloody motor started.

When I go to the track I was met with more giggles and people hiding their faces and Denys saying to me 'ah you made it then'.

This kind of practical joking was very much the norm in grand prix teams and you just had to take it and get on with life with a smile.

The rest of the weekend was for me really enjoyable though Team Suzuki in all its forms didn't have a great weekend

It was just a few short weeks later when I think it all sunk in as to how my life had changed at the British GP weekend in July 1981. We had a double decker bus with awning and catering for invited Suzuki dealers which was placed on the inside of the first corner. If you remember it was the weekend of Prince Charles' wedding to Lady Diana Spencer. The weather was amazing and the country basked in both the really hot sunshine and a rare moment of pomp and circumstance. They actually got married on the Friday which was the 31st of July and the GP was on Sunday 2nd August. I have no recollection of where we stayed for the weekend but for sure it would have been along with many other teams close to the circuit as possible. On the Friday morning I was at the circuit bright and early, an exception from my normal routine as this being the British GP my duties were somewhat more demanding.

I remember standing at the start of the pit lane watching the riders coming round the final bend in the first practice session. The sun was warm, the crowd sparse though still vocal, the full complement of SGB and GP riders were there including Huewen, Mamola, Crosby and others from the Italian squad and life felt very very good. The atmosphere was building and there was a buzz in the air that you only get at your home GP. Even when there was nothing on track happening on that Friday there was always that addictive sound of two stroke racing engines being revved in the paddock a few hundred yards away. It really didn't get any better than this.

Graeme Crosby stuck it on pole which was a fantastic achievement and probably sealed his move away from Suzuki to Yamaha for the following season. Jack Middleburg won the race from Kenny Roberts and in third place was Randy Mamola who also shared fastest lap with Kork Ballington. But the race was marred by Crosby, Huewen and Sheene failing to finish so it never really hit the highlights of the famous race there two years before. It was more famous for the fact that Croz had chucked it down the road on lap three taking out Sheene and Luchinelli.

CHIMAY 1981

As I mentioned previously Georges Annuzet, the chef de la fete de Chimay, the chairman of the motorcycle club and events director for the town had rather cleverly asked me to be the British rider representative or co-ordinator for the 1981 event. Clever in as much as I had no idea what he really wanted and was flattered to be asked. I suspect that in previous years he had done the leg work and the idea of having a Brit doing it from this end made a lot of sense. I know Georges and Barry were quite close friends. Barry had raced at Chimay for some years with a healthy start money arrangement that suited both men very handsomely. George also got one of the world's greatest ever riders on the list and could milk the ticket sales and publicity to the max. That was all well and good, but by the time the event came around, and my commitment to the Chimay event planning was required I was heavily employed by SGB and would find the time to organise things a very difficult commodity to find. But I had given my word and got stuck in.

Most communication with Georges was done via a fax machine. I would send him the proposed list of British riders with their class and costs and he would reply with a confirmation and thus I could move through and get the riders confirmed. Once we had the basic list sorted out and agreed he asked me to come over to meet him and the organising committee to finalise everything. They agreed that I could come over one weekend so as not to intrude on my work and also asked if I could ask the Suzuki grand prix team if they would like to add Chimay to their list on non-championship events for the year. That would mean Randy and Graeme Crosby riding against Barry. I asked Rex but the answer was a firm and very polite 'no'. Rex explained they were never going to add one off events to the already busy calendar. It also virtually coincided with the French GP so for SGB it was a no go.

So off I set in my little light blue Ford Fiesta over to Belgium. Sounds much harder than it was because once across the channel the open and hardly used roads meant easy and quick driving to Chimay. The committee had very kindly paid for my travel and a hotel room. So we met later in that afternoon or early evening around a large table in a local bar with papers and rider pictures etc laid out in front of us. Little food seemed to be forthcoming but they did keep the very splendid Belgium beer flowing. I am not really certain the trip was necessary, except to meet everyone face to face, but we sorted out the list and payments and had a very happy few hours together. So happy was it that I got completely pissed and fell over as I opened the door to my car! Not to worry as my fall to the gravel was applauded loudly. The next morning after a coffee fuelled breakfast with the boys again I set off back to UK.

For the event itself everything went smoothly and as far as I can recall there were no issues whatsoever with riders and travel/tickets/passes etc.

It must have been on the Friday during one of the warm-up sessions for the non 500 riders that a strange happening occurred between myself and Barry. The paddock though full to the brim with competitors' vans and caravans etc was strangely devoid of people. It was eerily quiet as I took a gently stroll around the grassy field that doubled as Race Central over the weekend. Up to that point I don't think I'd seen Barry to talk to. His caravan and vans etc were assembled very neatly in possibly the best position in the paddock but there was no one about as I wandered closer to them. As I drew level with the ensemble the caravan door flew open and Barry called me over in a sort of loud and sheepish whisper 'Ian Ian come here. Come and see this. Quick, before Steph gets back'. He was waving a magazine in his hand. He virtually dragged me inside his caravan sat down at the table and beckoned me to join him. Then he flashed the magazine but not before checking out the window to see that Steph wasn't about the come charging in. He seemed like a little schoolboy, desperate, almost bursting at the seams, to tell me something. His little face was split ear to ear with the biggest Barry grin ever.

'Look at this Ian' as he laid out the very latest edition of Men Only magazine on the table. 'Steph's gone shopping but if she comes back in you take the magazine and pretend it's yours ok?' I was really confused by all this. Here I was sitting in Barry's caravan with the man and about to be shown something which I guessed involved a naked woman, and he was as excited as 12 year old school boy at Christmas.

He flicked quickly to a double page spread of a beautiful blonde girl showing her very lovely wares. All Barry could say at that point was 'There's nine pages of her. Look' as he flicked page after page of this amazingly sexy girl. The penny still hadn't dropped but mainly due to the fact that I was sort of looking at her upside down or from the side at best.

And then he said it, actually he blurted it out. He knew this was the only chance he would get all weekend to show me and tell the story.

'It's her. Remember Nina from the Brands Hatch event? That girl you took to Brands. Well ever since you two stopped seeing each other I have been taking her out. I go up to her house in Orpington and we go out somewhere. I've been seeing her for months. Look at that body mate she's just gorgeous'.

He was sort of talking out loud but never really looking at me. He just kept his eyes glued to the pages, and there were plenty of them. I was shocked on so many levels but way too naïve to say anything at the time. We both ogled Nina, which was fine by me because actually I never did get to see her naked in the flesh, and he was buzzing about her and seeing her, behind Steph's back. I really didn't know what to say to Barry. Then he decided the risk was too great, folded the mag up and tucked it back under the seat. We chatted about a few other odds and sods for a minute or two and then I made my way back out into the hot sunshine. As I strolled further on around the paddock I rewound what had just happened and chuckled to myself. He was a monster where women were concerned. Possibly because I was young free and single I couldn't see much wrong with what he had done but at the same time his desperation not to be caught out by Steph showed how wrong he knew he had been.

A FUNNY THING
HAPPENED ON THE WAY
TO THE SPACE SHIP

Sometime later in Summer I got a phone call from Maurice Knight telling me to expect a call from the marketing department at Shell Oils in London. In those days they were based in Shell Mex House on the Strand just along from Charing Cross Station. Sure enough a short while later a guy called and explained that he needed a bike and rider for the day at a film shoot they were making for Shell Agricultural Oils up in Hertfordshire a week or so later. They needed the rider to look like a spaceman and had a complete silver suit for him to wear and wanted the Suzuki Katana because it looked very avant guard. Shell were a big sponsor of the team so of course we would do anything to help.

A day or so later the guy called back with a full briefing for me of what it was and where and asked if I would be coming and would I ride the bike. The answers were yes and no. But I had an idea of who could ride the bike. Damon Hill of course!

I had known Damon since his early bike racing days and knew that he was short of cash and eager to earn a few bob. So I called him, told him the story and agreed a fee for the day.

On the day of the shoot I collected him from his house somewhere in Wandsworth I think and off we set in the works Team Ford Transit with a bike and all some bits in case he dropped it. It was pissing with rain leaving some doubt about whether they would be able to shoot anything at all. However when we got to the farm where they were set up the weather had brightened considerably.

There was a massive film crew, catering van and motorhomes as if they were making Saving Private Ryan not a trade only Shell Oils infomercial.

Damon's job was to don all his spaceman kit, which looked surprisingly good, and ride off up the lane. The film crew would film his arrival in the shoddy old farm yard where he would meet the dishevelled old farmer who could of course benefit from using the new XYZ Shell Agri Oils product, which Damon would hand over to him before shooting off again on his space-like motorcycle.

All well and good but you can imagine our surprise and delight at finding out that the old farmer was in fact played by Melvyn Hayes from *It Ain't Half Hot Mum* the BBC hit comedy series about a British Army regiment in India. He was fantastic and very funny and friendly. As you may know on tv shoots of any sort there is a hell of a lot of waiting around so having someone like him for the day was a complete pleasure.

Mid to late afternoon our work was done, Damon did everything they wanted, so we toddled off back to Damon's house where we had tea and cake with his mum and sister before I returned to Beddington Lane.

I never saw the finished film but I know Shell were very pleased with what we did. Maurice was happy too. It just shows you what could, would and did happen in my life at SGB. I was growing used to the phrase 'expect the unexpected'.

I think I mentioned SGB Parts Director Eric Allvey's secretary Lynn. Well we became an item which opened my eyes to a couple of things. Firstly, SGB was a bit of a party place on the quiet. As soon as Lynn and I were an item party invites started to come in and so mid-week or on spare weekends we seemed to be at this staff member's house or another having a party. Or going on a Thursday night in a big group to a disco somewhere south of Croydon. It was in fact a great place to work, rest and play. The second thing was that despite Lynn being super lovely and very delicious, my spare time for a girlfriend was severely limited. Oh there was a third thing which I think I should get off my chest at last after all these years. Lynn couldn't drive and smashed up my brand new light blue Ford Fiesta. Sorry Denys but I couldn't let her take the blame so I told you it was me. Lynn lived with her parents quite close to SGB and so one evening after work we decided to pop out for fish and chips at the local parade of shops not a five minute drive away. Lynn persuaded me to let her drive which was all well and good until we started our descent into the bus lane to stop at the chippy. Some how she got confused and decided to park the car inside the bus shelter. One of those modern ones with a roof and a glass end panel...

We came to a grinding and very sudden halt and both headbutted the windscreen because, as you would expect, we weren't wearing our seat belts. Fortunately no real damage was done to us but the car looked very sorry for itself. Luckily SGB had a Mr Fix-it in the shape of Bill Ormsby who was responsible for cars, buildings, and all manner of other property matters. He sorted out a recovery truck and my dad came over to collect me. Boy did I feel like a prat the next day. I know Denys didn't believe me when I stated that it was definitely not Lynn driving. I made up some cock and bull story about kids cycling in front of me and having to swerve. Complete bollocks but as a gentleman I had to protect the lady's honour.

The Suzuki Katana was one of my favourite bikes and available in both 1000cc and 1100cc versions. The press only wanted to test the 1100cc bike which was understandable so that left the lonely 1000cc bike often unloved and sitting unused in the workshop. I decided to be its best friend and took it out as much as possible. It was a lovely bike from my perspective. Plenty of power but very usable and comfortable.

I really don't know where the idea came from but in about mid-October 1981 I put the idea to Denys that for some cheap extra publicity we could take three Katanas on the Beaujolais run down to Macon if France in mid November. Denys was always amenable to a mad idea especially if it was cheap and he jumped at the idea. So I had to get a few riders on board and was banned from taking any of the team riders for obvious reasons. Damon's name popped into my head but either he declined it or was too busy. Not sure which so I rounded up Club racing legend (a legend in his own lunchtime at least) Conor Brennan and budding motorcycling journo Matt Oxley.

If you don't know the Beaujolais run is a mad cap idea to bring a bottle or two of the new and completely horrid stuff back from the vineyards in Macon to central London and as always it's a race without it being allowed to be a race. You drift down through France on the 14th November and at midnight get your bottle or bottles to race the 500 odd miles back to London. On these bikes I thought we were guaranteed a win and national newspaper coverage. I was on the 1000cc best friend Katana and the other two were on the 1100cc bikes. Then Tom Waterer got involved and insisted that I at least wore Suzuki branded clothing. He was pushing a new line in over suits and riding outerwear. So I said yes. Big mistake because it was mainly crap and mainly unlined. On the way down, which was a very delightful all day pootle down through daylight hours I began having my doubts about this kit. At 100-120mph on the way back it was very obvious the kit was so bad and cold that it was dangerous. The other two, Conor and Matt were wrapped up properly and quicker riders than me anyway, so we decided to split and let them crack on. I found a sweet spot at about 90mph which I could bear but they were impossible for me to hang on to.

We knew it was a real race because there were a couple of Porsche 911s and an Audi UK Quattro all fully kitted out. On and off all the way back these guys would catch up and then we'd leave them again. We needed to stop more often for fuel but they weren't prepared to drive as mad fast as we were. Or should I say Conor and Matt were. I just plodded on at a respectable lick and got back to London a couple of hours later, very cold and determined to let Tom know what a load of old shit this clothing was.

I had expected us to win but found out later that Audi UK sort of cheated, or if one was kind, that they had a master plan. That plan went by the name of Stirling Moss. The legend that is Stirling had been retained by Audi and kept nice and warm and fresh in Dover waiting for their Quattro to appear off the earliest Calais ferry it could get on. When it appeared the driver switch took place and he literally flew off like a scalded cat up the A2 to London to steal all the publicity. I still think we might have won the day but he was bigger than us so that's all they, the media, needed.

About the same time I was asked to sit in a sales and marketing meeting in Maurice Knight's large office in the same building as my little office was located. He told me to sit at the back of the room and observe. With a few minutes to go before the meeting started people began to arrive, then some more people to fill the room. I would say there were fifteen of us all crammed in. Though Maurice had a large desk there was no meeting table so we just grabbed or brought a chair with us and found a spot to perch.

The gathering was made up of me, sitting quietly at the back, Tom Waterer, various sales reps, the advertising agency team, a technical bod or two and a secretary or two to take notes.

The main thrust of the meeting was to discuss the new bikes coming, in the near future, and look at the ads for them and key selling points for the sales team to develop and work on. Maurice was in full flow and very impressive to watch he was too. As the conversation developed someone mentioned that a particularly low end bike, it might have been a scooter or 125cc offering, would sell well 'because it's cheap'.

Maurice went into overdrive on this remark, though it was sometimes difficult to know if he was angry because sometimes when he was angry and letting rip he seemed to have an even bigger smile on his face than when he was being genuinely funny. 'Cheap, cheap' he bellowed. 'We don't do cheap bikes we do excellent value' was his response at about 110 decibels.

The ad agency boys then produced some mock up ads which were very good and which were discussed in some detail before the meeting ended just in time for some of them to enjoy a decent lunch.

LET'S GET BACK TO RACING

Again at a similar time about mid summer 1981 Maurice called me into his office for a chat. There were times when I was confused. You see Maurice was the senior of the two between him and Denys and yet Denys was MD of the bike division but was often not in meetings like this one. Denys was also effectively in charge of the racing activities of SGB, so I understood, yet Maurice was about to brief me on a couple of things that I expected Denys to be present on.

It was just Maurice and me in the office so I wasn't expecting much. I thought it was just a catch up on bits and pieces.

This is how it went:

Maurice –

'How you settling in with the team then?'

'Fine thanks Maurice'

'Good'

'I see you're taking lots of good pictures we can use in press stuff but I think we should get a dedicated photographer to follow the British team, so we have plenty of media friendly photos. What do you think?'

'Yes er of course Maurice'

'I want a proper record of our racing history so I have had a chat with this guy and I want you to go and meet him, have a proper chat with him and see what you think. He needs to be at all the events this year and get candid stuff and get really under the skin of the team. Here's his card and some of his work which he wants back. Go and see him will you and then report back to me'

Maurice gave me a bundle of pictures and a black portfolio folder for a guy called Malcolm Bryan.

Thinking that was it I got up to leave and started for the door but Maurice called me back sharpish.

'I'm not finished yet' It was a sort of funny sarcastic remark that Maurice was very good at without making the recipient, me, feel like a complete idiot.

'Do you still go to other race events Ian, ones that we the full team don't go to? National stuff?'

'Yes I am always at Brands and sometimes Snetterton when I have the chance'

'Good well this is totally confidential and it must stay that way. We are looking to get a bigger team together for next season and I want to look at a few riders. The problem is I cannot start appearing at these race events because it'll be obvious what I'm doing and start rumours and nonsense. So I want you to do it for me.'

'Here's a list of riders that I think are worth watching'

At that point he slid a hand-written list of about five names on a piece of office paper across his desk to me.

'I need you to watch them closely. See how they look, present themselves, are they professional, would they make the grade in a full time race team. You know what we want. Assume a watching brief over the next few meetings you can get to and report back to me in confidence. Make sure you don't discuss these names with anyone else and if you need tickets for paddock and pits to anything let me know and I'll sort them out. I don't want to know their results because I can get than from MCN. I want to know if you think they have that special something and professional attitude'

'Oh and don't wear any Suzuki clothing to these meetings because that'll just draw too much attention. If anyone you know asks what you are doing there just tell them you are having a weekend off or something like that' Maurice's big smile was all over his face. With that I left the room and across the landing to my office a bit shocked and confused.

Did Maurice Knight just ask me to scout some riders for him for the following season. Riders who would be offered professional terms and a position in the Suzuki GB racing team alongside Keith Huewen etc? Well actually he did...

I remember sitting down to think about this in between phone calls and the usual non stop stuff that was everyday life in the office. I was really excited but up to that point hadn't even looked at the names on the list.

Now you might be interested in the five names on the list but I think it would be wrong of me to reveal them all because they might blame me for their non appearance in the SGB team for 1982. In any case I think that the list should remain private but I will reveal the two names who did get in the team.

Paul Iddon and Mark Boughton.

I knew who they both were but didn't know them as friends or anything. So armed with my list and fully pit passed up off I went to a number of race events over the next month or two. It was like the old days in the Bemsee times. I seemed to know so many people that it became hard to find the time to watch the guys in the paddock and pits in between chatting with old friends like Conor Brennan who would take the piss relentlessly. Conor was about the only one who guessed what I was up to. He was an astute fellow. He knew I wasn't there because I was bored or wasn't getting enough racing fixes at SGB.

Now it would be wrong of me to claim any credit for Mark and Paul getting into the team for 1982. My role was to observe them both, and the other three as well, from a professional standpoint not whether they could win anything much. Over the following few weeks I went to as many meetings as possible where they were riding and kept my eye on them. I took a look from inside the pits and the paddock, tried to watch both their own presentation and that of those around them. How did the vans look, how did they treat fans for autographs and the like. Both Mark and Paul were of course at that time quite low key but they had their fans and followers. I don't think I actually spoke to either of them except for a hello or 'how ya doing' kind of thing and certainly I never spoke to any of the five about what I was actually doing.

I knew quite a few of Mark Boughton's friends and colleagues because he was what I would have described as part of the south London bike racing mafia. By that I mean he was good friends with the London racing fraternity like Gary

Lingham and related guys like Rob Myers and the like. That wasn't a problem at all but it meant that if I was lingering near Mark it was inevitable that someone I knew would come for a chat.

Maurice didn't want any recommendations from me as to who he should hire but more of an overview. I didn't score or rate them either. I didn't produce a list in order of who I thought would fit in. My report to Maurice was verbal and done in his office one morning. He didn't ask who I would want in the team from a PR point of view but did want to know who I thought was good at PR and presentation. That was an easy answer because Mark Boughton had it all going on. He was good looking in a Boy Band kind of way, was photogenic and very approachable and articulate with it.

That was it. I made my thoughts known to Maurice and we didn't speak again until later in the season when he told me he had nearly made his mind up. He then told me it was likely to be Mark and Paul for the following season but of course I should say nothing.

One of the reasons perhaps that Paul Iddon was on that list given to me by Maurice was that he had been to Maurice's office one day without an appointment, in an effort to at least shake his hand and get his face known. Paul was racing in the ACU Marlboro Clubman's Championship on a Suzuki GSX1100 and would often drive down to Suzuki GB to collect spare parts. On one of these trips he presented himself to Maurice and offered to ride for nothing the following season if Suzuki would back him with a decent bike. Paul did indeed of course get SGB backing for the 1982 season on the ill-fated Katana 1100 in the MCN Streetbike Series. The bike was not competitive so Suzuki quickly pulled the plug. Paul told me he was sure things would end there but in fact Maurice rustled up a stock RG500 for the season in various different events. The only issue was that Maurice, being a canny tight wad, took up Paul's offer to do it for nothing!

On a separate note, but one Paul wanted to discuss with me, was the strange case of the gearboxes of the Suzuki GSXR750 which he and Neil Robinson rode in 1986. Very tragically Neil Robinson died at Scarborough in September 1986. There had been some concern among the riders about the gearboxes on this bike potentially causing accidents. Officially this was never acknowledged but privately Paul and others in the team had concerns. No proof exists of course but it was a point Paul has felt very strongly about ever since. Paul put it this way when we spoke on the issue

'Both myself & Chris Martin had the bikes lock up (only once), his at Donington, resulting in a crash breaking his elbow, mine at Hockenhiem on my very first lap of practice going into the first chicane. On each occasion the mechanics didn't find anything wrong with them & I never had an issue again. I privately thought it was possible that Neil Robinson may have had the same issue at Scarborough resulting in his tragic crash. I asked the 1987 mechanics to examine the gearbox in the 86/87 closed season & they found that in certain circumstances the gearbox could 'over select' causing it to lock up.'

At some point during the 81 season Rex White asked me about coming to Ireland for the Ulster GP. To be honest I don't think I even knew about the race. I certainly had no idea it was in Dundrod or where Dundrod is on a map. Rex explained that it would be really helpful if I could go because given that it was northern Ireland and during the height of the troubles they would have to leave much earlier in the week and would definitely need spares and equipment brought over. The only issue would be that I needed to fly from Heathrow to Belfast so my baggage capacity would be limited.

Before I knew it I was issued with a ticket. I would leave on the Thursday lunchtime from Heathrow to Belfast and be met at the airport by 'Big John'.

Like a lot of people my age I am somewhat scarred by the Northern Ireland troubles. Us British had watched in horror as bombs and shootings became a thing of horrific regularity on the evening news. So I have to say my first visit to Belfast made me a little bit concerned. I had visited Eire quite a few times as my father's family were from Dublin so I know a thing or two about Irish hospitality and how things can get a wee bit boisterous. I do remember sitting on the old prop plane at Heathrow thinking would we even get that far and who the hell was 'Big John'? It did also cross my mind that he might be security for the team. Did we even have security?

Arriving at Belfast airport was a shock in itself. The troubles came starkly home right there and then because all the windows and interior glass partitions etc had been covered up with plywood sheeting. Walking through the normal glass corridors in an airport is a bright and interesting experience. Here in Belfast airport it was like being inside a shoe box or worse.

It was then that my concerns became very real as I heard my name being called out over the public address system. It was loud and everyone could hear it 'Would Mr Ian Burgess, recently arrived from London Heathrow please make his way to the car hire reception area where his party awaits him'.

I don't know why but that just seemed like a trap to me. My little IRA conscious mind was thinking in overdrive as I plodded through the airport pushing a baggage trolly piled high with my bag and loads of brown cardboard boxes and bubble wrapped parts.

But as I arrived there he was 'Big John'. He was big too. Very tall with if I remember a decent beard on him and a huge smile. He shook my hand so hard it nearly fell off. We loaded the car and sped off into the back woods of Ulster, down country lanes at break-neck speed. When we got close to the circuit, which by the way if you don't know is a road circuit in and around the tiny Ulster village of Dundrod, the traffic built up somewhat but Big John never queued he just drove up to the Police road blocks past all the queuing cars etc and announced to the Policemen standing there 'I have ya man from Suzuki in the back'. I don't know if he was one of them or they knew him another way but miraculously we were waived through and into the paddock we arrived. The sun was shining and things were looking pretty good. Team SGB were nicely set up at the back of the paddock area. Big John unloaded all the boxes and then disappeared again but not before telling me he would be my driver for the weekend, and would see me at the hotel the following morning.

I felt rather odd standing there. I had no idea who Big John was, where I was exactly, where or what hotel I was staying in and felt somewhat exposed. It didn't last long because the one thing you find out very quickly when racing in Ireland is that paddock marshals and gate security seemed to be nonexistent. The public get in everywhere. It was so bad that the first thing Rex White told me was to keep everything locked and tucked up because they'll pinch anything they can get their hands on. For example the flaps to the team truck awning were always shut tight and bikes etc were never left outside. Truck and van doors always locked.

It's not that the Irish are a bunch of untrustworthy thieves, not a bit, it's just that they are starved of top flight bike racing and many cannot possibly afford to come over to the UK or even the Isle of Man to see it. Thus when the circus comes to town they go mad for it.

The sunny skies disappeared to be replaced with heavy rain for most of the weekend. The hotel we were all at seemed to be a kind of motel affair with a bar and dance hall arrangement attached to it. Some of us tried to get a beer but that was fraught, as there were quite possibly several hundred drinkers crammed in tight all as thirsty as hell and a complete dearth of bar staff. People were shouting and hollering at the few bar staff to get a beer.

The next morning Big John was there on time waiting for me to get out the door. Once again we sped off not stopping for any queues and announcing to the waiting Police at the checkpoints that he had that man from Suzuki in the back.

The rain was, if anything, worse than previously so I sheltered in the team bus and under the zipped up awning where the rain belted down making a huge noise on the roof. All of a sudden I noticed a little hand appear under the awning bottom rail. It was digging away at the gravel and dirt making a big enough hole like a trench almost for a young lad's head to appear. The lad was about 15 maybe and though totally dirty and wet sported a massive smile. You have to imagine this next bit in a broad northern Irish accent if you can. The lad wriggled and pushed so he could get his head and one shoulder through, looked up at me and said 'have you got any stickers?' I was astonished. We all screamed out laughing but his effort was well rewarded as I filled his grubby hands with stickers and team pictures etc. He then wriggled his way back out again and that was him done.

Rex immediately observed dryly 'you better fill that hole up or they'll all be coming through'.

The Ulster GP was a great experience. The passion for racing was everywhere. The crowds turn up in massive numbers and the atmosphere was incredible, but when you get back to the airport there was a huge sense of relief.

At this point I am going to list all the riders who were at Suzuki GB in one way or another during my time there. They were all a pleasure to deal with and though I wouldn't claim any of them was more helpful to me than the others some were overly conscious of the role press and media management can help them and thus went the extra mile to deliver.

There has been much written about and discussed regarding the Graeme Crosby and Randy Mamola pairing. The infamous cup of pee incident and general claimed dislike between them. If I am honest I never saw that but then again I rarely saw them together let alone talking together. Graeme was always super generous with his time and very friendly. When he left Suzuki for Yamaha he came up to my office with Big Mick his mechanic and personally gave me a set of his racing leathers from 1981. I didn't ask for them and was taken aback at this gesture. I had thought riders kept helmets and leathers. On that particular subject I am going to make something quite clear. Some years ago Graeme contacted me to ask if I still had the leathers and could he have them back because he was getting all his racing memorabilia together for a display. I told him that when I was selling the family home, due to divorce, they were still in a bag in the loft. Furthermore that my ex-wife was in the house, I had moved to France and so he should ask her. She then apparently told Graeme that I had taken them with me to France. That is a lie. They were in the loft and I suspect she had got rid of them and didn't have the balls to tell him. There, I feel better now. Sorry about that Graeme but I really didn't have them old chap.

Keith Huewen was always fun and someone I classed as a friend. I had known him for a few years before. I went to his house near Northampton several times, went for lunatic rides with him driving his 2.8 litre Capri and if anyone knew the benefit of press coverage it was Keith.

Randy was an odd one at the time. He was full of intent, talent and commitment but had few social skill and even less to say. I spoke to him on occasion but he was nothing like the enthusiastic and verbose character you see and hear today on the television. I liked him though and probably had more to do with his manager Jim Doyle, an ex Pan Am pilot and decorated US Airforce pilot, so I believe. He was a very nice guy who I met many years later at one of the German motorcycle trade shows, and he remembered me. I was staggered but he did.

Then of course there was John Newbold. I have written a complete chapter about the fateful weekend at the North West 200 in 1982. But suffice to say at this point John was a gentleman. Calm, quiet, not up himself in any way and easy to like and get along with.

So here's the list. Of course I will return to some of the riders later in the book;

- Paul Iddon
- Mark Boughton
- Keith Huewen
- Graeme Crosby
- Randy Mamola
- Mick Grant
- Roger Marshall
- John Newbold
- Rob McElnea
- Barry Sheene

Plus I would give a little shout out to a couple of riders from other teams, Suzuki and not, who I met, liked and had respect for. Some were a little bit after my Suzuki days but when I was active in motorcycle marketing.

Franco Uncini, Wayne Gardner, Virginio Ferrari, Gary Lingham, Kevin Schwantz.

It's also worth noting as a conclusion to the Maurice Knight 'we need a team photographer' moment with Malcolm Bryan that I did indeed do as Maurice instructed and go and chat with Malcolm. He lived near Brands Hatch with his lovely wife Monica.

Malcolm was indeed a very talented photographer who took inspiration from the famous Observer sports snapper

Eamonn McCabe. McCabe's ability to show an unguarded or special moment from a unique angle and with texture and feel was his unique and winning trade mark, and which won him many an award.

Malcolm started working for the SGB team immediately that summer and followed it through in '82. He was a typical photographer who had not much to say for himself as his camera did the talking but was fine company and never stopped watching the subject to capture some moments and record the ups and downs of the team. Some of his pics are included in the photo section and I am grateful that he was with us.

Very few people will know this but Malcolm was also fundamental to the development of digital photography. In the years after he left us camera makers were already thinking and developing ideas for digital even before the internet came along. They knew there was a new age in photography and digital was it. Malcolm had been covering the Paris - Dakar rally and had I think always used Canon cameras. They contacted him and contracted him to cover the rally as per normal but using a helicopter they provided to get him in and out of special sections equipped with a laptop and a new camera that used a microchip instead of film. The pictures were then downloaded onto the laptop for later use. Of course there were many other drivers in the race for the technology and understanding but Malcolm played a small part in that effort.

I need to say a few words about Graeme Crosby at this point. Graeme was and still is a true gentleman. An honest, funny, hard working and very fast rider who probably doesn't get the recognition he deserves. But if you look at his post-race life you'll see that perhaps the one source of respect that could mean more to any factory rider and which has more weight to it than any other, the factory itself, loves Graeme. He is still invited to Heritage events in japan and many other places, he still rides the old bikes that he competed on and is held in high esteem and with much affection by the factory. During my time with Graeme in 1981 he was always smiling, never had any precious moments, would always listen to me and always always talk to the media with no hesitation and with interest and respect. At the end of the season when he was about to leave he threw a little pub piss-up for the team in a pub near Sevenoaks. He arrived in his pride and joy a black Jaguar XJS, which he went on to ship back to New Zealand. There were perhaps ten of us there and typical of Graeme it was calm and fairly quiet. Beers were drunk, things were said and then well before closing time we all left to see Graeme and wife drive off into the sunset. Actually it was a dark and wet night by the time we left the pub but I didn't want to let the truth spoil a good story. A week or so before leaving Suzuki GB he and his mechanic 'Big Mick' came to my office one morning to have a chat. Apart from the sad goodbye stuff he said some very nice things about working with me which was unexpected and lovely to hear, but then he stepped out of the office and came back with a holdall from which he produced a pair of his race leathers from that year. 'I want you to have these Ian. A gift, a thank you'. I was speechless and immensely grateful because what went behind that gift was worth far more to me than the leathers themselves, as fantastic as they were. In the 1982 season Croz went to Yamaha to race in the Agostini team and proved his credentials, to any doubters of his two stroke abilities, by finishing second in that year's championship.

SUZUKI GOES SOUTH!

Late in 1981 I got a phone call from Edna Calder, PJ's right-hand lady. She worked in an office next to PJ's on the executive landing of the old Victorian villa I also worked in on Beddington Lane. I would often see Edna during the week but she rarely talked to me on a business level. She was always engaging and very supportive but her remit didn't really include PR and my little marketing bureau for the Suzuki brand, and certainly she never got involved with the racing side of the business.

I walked across the landing to her office at the agreed time that same afternoon wondering what on earth she could want me for. Perhaps it was something outside the Suzuki GB arena because as I mentioned before she and PJ had a number of other business interests.

Her secretary showed me into her little office which had a connecting door to PJ's which she suddenly walked up to and opened beckoning me to follow. Into PJ's grand suite we went. I hadn't been in this office before and wasn't sure if PJ was in that day. It was as usual a little intimidating because PJ was a dominant force to come up against. Luckily he was out so we sat down in a couple of armchairs and I waited with my pen and notebook at the ready.

Edna was always softly spoken but very precise in what she said. She measured her words carefully, as if she had rehearsed them.

'Ian I'm going to tell you something that is confidential and which at this stage cannot be repeated to anyone not even your secretary. You are one of just a few people outside the board who have been told this and I need it to stay that way. Do I make myself clear?'.

'Yes Edna of course'. I could tell by that something big was coming but not this big.

'I want you to meet me tomorrow morning at a Crawley industrial estate. Gatwick Road to be precise. You'll get the instructions in a moment. I can tell you now that next spring Suzuki GB will be moving to a purpose-built facility in Crawley. We need you to look at it and understand what is happening there. I need you to start to prepare for the opening and launch and all the related press and media work required. You and I will form a small committee reporting to PJ. You and I will be responsible for the entire opening events of the headquarters of Suzuki GB and the internal staff communications. Are you ok with that Ian?'.

I was completely wrong footed by this. Of all the things she could have told me this was not on the list. It hadn't even crossed my mind that Beddington Lane, the iconic and perhaps famous address for Suzuki in the UK would be no more.

Edna's secretary came into the room with a slip of paper for me. It showed a little map of the location with the address.

'How about 10am tomorrow Ian can you make that?'.

That actually wasn't a question it was an Edna instruction. So I answered in the positive and left. My secretary Sue was gasping to know what our meeting was all about mainly because it had to be important if Edna wanted me, and she knew it. All I could tell her was I couldn't tell her anything and I wouldn't be in until at least lunchtime the following day. Sue was so excited she was begging me to tell her 'Come on, come on tell what's going on', but I couldn't.

So, quite early the next day I set off from home in Bexley around the M25 and down the M23 towards Brighton but turning off at junction 10 to go into the industrial estate of Crawley and onto the Gatwick Road. At the second small roundabout on the right hand side was a massive building site with a small car park area inside which already was Edna's car. I wasn't late at all, that would not be acceptable to her or me, but she was just there before me.

She was in her element, smiling and marching off giving me massive amounts of detail that I couldn't possibly remember and with a couple from the senior architect and contractor team with us, she gave me the full tour. The building was largely up but not fitted out at all. The roof was on and the staircases were in but little else was done. It was huge and now having walked all around it and having the foresight to bring my trusty old SGB camera with me, to get some early snaps, she gave me the detail as much as she could at that point.

It's impossible for me to recall whether this first meeting was end of 1981 or very early 1982, certainly it was winter and nowhere near springtime. Edna declared that the moving date would be late March or very early April. That I would be responsible for the complete press/pr and guests arrival and management and tours of the building and those guests would include many of the richest and most infuential people in the business world. Also that the building would be opened by Gerald Ronson and his wife Gail so it must run like clock work or Gerald will explode.

I was very excited by all of this. It seemed to make some very good business sense to group all Suzuki and one or two other brands under one roof and the location was an excellent one. Great railway connections to London and a fabulous airport literally on the doorstep and easy in and out by motorway. The work force on site seemed to be in the hundreds but probably it was only sixty to seventy. Deliveries were coming all the time we were there so quite clearly they knew there was a deadline that would have penalties attached for missing.

We agreed to meet the next day in her office for an update of the project and she made it clear that over the next few months I needed to be committed to this project. I was still concerned though that it was top secret which would have some problems for me when planning anything.

Edna went off for another meeting and so I took the chance to have another wander around the place on my own. Of course at that stage there was no way of knowing how the final layout would be and no chance of knowing where my office would be, but all in all I was bursting with excitement and also feeling the pressure already. Pressure that would rise and rise in the coming months.

On the way back to the office where I would once again tell Sue nothing about where I had been I realised that I was being asked once more to take on more and more work with no extra pay. It didn't bother me much but they didn't pay me much anyway so though this was great chance to add to my experience I felt I should get another thousand or so. It never happened.

I had to tell Sue something because she knew I was up to some secret squirrel work with Edna. So I just said that I was working on a project for the company that I would tell her about very soon but at that time I wasn't able to say a thing to anyone. She was fine; she had been there long enough to know that there were always 'projects' happening and those involved were not allowed to say anything.

At the meeting with Edna the flowing meeting her attitude softened greatly towards me. She was finally able to get on with the planning for the opening and seemed to enjoy being able to share info with me. It was decided that we should make the staff announcement asap and I would create a staff newspaper called Lock Stock and Barrel all about the move to Crawley. The issue was to tell people early enough for them to understand what was happening and decide if they wanted to come to Crawley or find another job. Key staff and all the directors wouldn't be a problem of course, but many other office staff might not want to work so far from home. It was also decided that I would tell Sue which turned out to be a problem because she almost immediately told me she wouldn't make the move to Gatwick Road. I was quite shocked but in reality Sue was a home girl who liked the convenience of working close to home without much of a commute. Never the less I was gutted to be losing my wing man. I have never disliked change but so much of it in a short space of time could be very disruptive.

A few days later I got a call from Denys to pop down and see him in his office. As soon as I was inside and the door closed Denys asked me if I knew Virginio Ferrari. I had to admit that though I had spoken to him once or twice in passing I knew little about him. He seemed very likeable though.

That seemed to please Denys because he then announced that Virginio was coming back to Suzuki the following year and would be in the office the next day. I was required to take Virginio to our favourite park just up the road in Wallington and take a few PR shots of him.

Sure enough the following day I heard that Virginio was downstairs with Denys who it was rumoured had put together a big money deal with a tobacco firm to sponsor the team. I went down to the office a little later with my camera and had a chat with Virginio and Denys. Virginio was a great guy, always smiling and happy. You may remember he had a cheeky little boy face under a mop of black curly hair. He spoke reasonable English too. We seemed to get along just fine. He couldn't stop asking me questions as we went out to the Team workshop at the back. Then Denys gave me the keys to I think PJ's Porsche 928 so we could take some more stylish and relaxed shots at the park.

Off we toddled for the five minute drive to the park where I took loads of pics with Virginio in a Suzuki jacket posing by the car etc. Less than an hour later I brought him back to Denys where I think they signed a contract and he was sent back to Italy. All in a day's work so it seemed. I was mistaken in thinking that Virginio was already a Suzuki rider but in fact he had left Suzuki two seasons before to set up the Cagiva grand prix project with the factory. It had been a disaster for everyone so he was quickly scooped up back into the Suzuki family.

Moving Suzuki GB, a multi brand and multi product business with several hundred employees and all the stores, equipment and support was never going to be easy or quick. Our entire attention was focussed on the move and preparing for it and the official opening event that would follow soon after. When I say everything was focussed on it I mean that we gave 100% to our day job and then another 100% to the move and its implications.

As for me I would spend many an hour driving to, from and at the new Gatwick Road site watching it develop and shape from the muddy building site as was on my first visit to a pristine new office and warehouse headquarters building with the spiffing showroom type entrance area, grassed frontage and masses of parking along each side. The race team would be housed bottom left just back from the front offices which ran all along the front over the two floors and along the right hand side of the building.

A major transformation was in place because HB tobacco had come on board for the GP team bringing with them, depending on which 'inside source' you chose to believe, somewhere between $800,000 and $4m a year. Tobacco companies had long been involved with motorsport with Marlboro being the most famous. They were all awash with cash and had to find a home for some of it which would maintain that youth audience and brand strength which were very important to them.

The other change was that the GP team was now split away from the direct control of SGB in that it would now be run as a GP team outside the buildings of SGB as had been the case for many years. It would be run by Garry Taylor who for some years had worked for the Suzuki advertising agency, Brandmark, and his girlfriend Deborah Shenton. If I am honest she seemed to have more GP team experience than Garry because her dad was Stan Shenton who had run Triumph's racing set up in the late sixties and had been the Team manager/Director behind the massively successful Team Kawasaki with riders like Mick Grant and Barry Ditchburn and of course winning multiple world titles in 250 and 350 world titles with Kork Ballington on board.

For the very short term they would be based at the new Gatwick Road race workshops while they sorted out their new facilities somewhere else. That somewhere else turned out to be Edenbridge in Kent because they found a super little workshop arrangement behind the John Surtees Renault dealership and also because Gary and Deborah lived just outside Edenbridge. Most convenient.

The warehouse part of the Gatwick Road set-up was hugely bigger than I had expected yet it still didn't hold any stock of bikes. Bikes were still held in Westbury , Wiltshire and distributed from there. Gradually as the weeks ticked by towards the moving in date of late March the place was finished off with carpet, offices appearing from nowhere, concreting of access drives, lighting and landscaping. I even had to get a photographer down there late one evening to get some shots of the place fully lit up with bikes in the entrance lobby and floodlights picking out the length and breadth of the huge building.

Back at Beddington Lane every office and department was working out of boxes and packing cases as we seemed to rush headlong into the move to Gatwick Road. The move actually took place over a week or so that teething roubles could be identified and overcome. As for my office well it seemed to have been overlooked. I didn't have one or hadn't been allocated one in the short term. That didn't matter so much as I was on the move constantly.

One of the key parts of the forthcoming grand opening day was dividing the guests into smaller groups to be guided around the whole facility before they enjoyed a slap up lunch. In order to do this we got about five of the secretaries from the directors into a car or two and off we went to Debenhams or one like it in Croydon to sort them out with a new and very smart wardrobe for the day. They had been briefed by Edna as to what was suitable, but the final choice was theirs. I was equipped with a very large wad of cash and told to sort things out in store. In fact it went quite well. The girls seemed to be having a ball. They found exactly what they wanted, and I simply sorted out the bill at the end.

By mid-March the racing season had started so together with my two days jobs and weekends away racing things were in overload territory. But it all worked out quite well. Paul Iddon and Mark Boughton were on board and doing quite well. Keith Huewen was to do all the British Championship rounds plus selected GPs and of course new boy Virginio Ferrari joined Randy Mamola in the charge on the 500 GP world championship in the newly formed Team HB Suzuki.

So it was good bye to Beddington Lane, which seemed to happen with barely a tear and no fanfare or even a look back over our collective shoulder, and a big HELLO to Gatwick Road, Crawley. It was new, it was big and it was all very shiny. We moved in and though the seating plan changed a few times very quickly for some, it seemed to go very well. A coach or two would scoop up those coming from Croydon each morning and bring them down and back again after work but inevitably we lost quite a few along the way who didn't fancy that kind of change. I don't blame them but with them went some of the identity of SGB in my opinion. Among them was of course Sue my secretary and the one and only Derek Goatley, the man who drank more than his fare share, invented the Goatley Shuffle and never stopped cracking jokes. Also about then Bill Ormsby who was in charge of all things property, cars, and maintenance decided to hold off from leaping over.

All in all the company had changed. How could it not when the old was a bunch of mismatched offices and cubby holes across two and a half locations and the new was a purpose built and very large new office establishment quite a distance south of Croydon?

I must say a quick word about yet another brand we seemed to collect along the way during 1981; Bell Helmets. Not sure exactly when it was but perhaps mid to late summer that year I was told that PJ and Maurice had acquired the UK distribution company for Bell Helmets. The company was based in south London near Tooting Common I think. It was run by the gently spoken Scot, David Valentine and I was, yes you've guessed it, to take over the PR and marketing support function of the brand. No problem at all because as you know I had slightly less than fuck all to do during the working week...

I was instructed to go and meet David and his small team and find out what they had been doing in the marketing and publicity area, get to know the products and take it on. In fact they were nice people who had done a reasonable job and while the product wasn't as strong as I had hoped you surely could not fail with a brand like Bell, could you? Bell had quite possibly one of the best ad campaigns in the US ever when they ran the ad headline – IF YOU'VE GOT A TEN DOLLAR HEAD WEAR A TEN DOLLAR HELMET. Just brilliant!

So Gatwick Road was up and running although full of boxes, people not sure where to go and me planted in the main office downstairs in amongst the car boys, technical chaps and the sales teams. It wasn't going to work and it didn't. I was told a new cubby hole would be found for me after the grand opening the following week.

I need to paint the scene here before explaining how the grand opening actually went. It would be a normal working day and the whole building would be taken over for a massive opening event where captains of industry, business leaders, dignitaries and more millionaires and their chauffeurs would assemble that day than anywhere else in the UK.

Staff were briefed, senior secretaries were suited and booted and had rehearsed their routes and guidance scripts, chauffeur food and facilities were arranged, the podium and small stage were in position in the large entrance hall, everything was cleaned and sorted. Media and journos were there too in some number. I had to prepare the list for the motorcycle trade and vet the other lists from each department.

All in all I would guess there were about 100 guests but to be honest it could have been two hundred, the place seemed to be crawling with people on that very bright and sunny morning of April 2nd 1982. Not sure of the actual date but that one rings a loud bell in my head.

Oh and Gerald Ronson and wife Gail would do the honours of opening the building formally from the stage where he would make a short speech. No pressure there then.

Yes we were owned by Heron Corporation but up until a few weeks before the opening day I had never had anything to do with Heron, which were based on the Euston Road just east of Madame Tussaud's. Ronson was famous for being a hard business man and task master and also owning the number plate RR1 which he proudly displayed on his Roller. I was way down the pecking order and would never normally have expected to talk to Gerald Ronson or indeed anyone in Heron headquarters. However, his assistant executive secretary, a lady I think who was called Diane was either given me as a contact point or found out my name due to the invite list I was adding to and began to call me, on the odd occasion to check details with and ask about certain things for the day.

A few days before the event she called me and announced that Gerald would not be making a speech because he doesn't like making them. I remember being surprised at this because surely that would be known well in advance wouldn't it? She told me that Gail, Ronson's wife, would make the speech instead. She then called me again just before the event and asked about catering and facilities for all the chauffeurs. 'It's very important, Ian, to take care of the chauffeurs because if we don't word will get back to their bosses and we'd be in the dog house'. To be fair she wasn't the only one to mention how important it is to look after the drivers. I assured her we had a special room for them to relax, with loads of comfy chairs, television and their own catering team.

She then went on the make a point that PJ had 'already been told' that Gerald wants to make a walk-round inspection of the whole building before the main event gets going, and that even though he is with PJ and perhaps other directors someone else should be with them to make notes of what Gerald says, because he will have changes and issues which will need to be dealt with without a follow up. In actual fact my work on the day was fairly slight apart from looking after media so I had been told already that I was to follow Gerald and the team around the building and make notes of everything he said.

Really that was a very easy job. I just needed to write the word FUCK down a lot because fuck me does Gerald Ronson swear. He charged off at quite a pace with us almost shuffling along after him and he kicked doors open saying 'for fuck's sake put kick plates on every door', and 'that floor is fucking useless get it replaced' and the like. He was, it seemed, a very unhappy and angry man. Probably all a show but he did it well.

The guests arrived in a constant stream of Rollers and 500 S Class Mercedes, journalists and guests were guided and toured the building hopefully impressed as they trotted around and then the assembled masses gathered in the reception lobby for the speeches.

I had noticed Gail Ronson earlier. I cannot say I have met or even been close to many billionaires and their wives but they certainly have a thing about them. They ooze style, money, exquisite presentation, make up and aura. She had it all going on but was wearing a rather odd wrap around green gown affair. It was clearly an expensive and unique piece and certainly she wouldn't be lost in a crowd but I'm not sure it suited her entirely.

Gail Ronson is a very attractive lady, make no mistake. Ronson, it was said, loved her so much he named his second Super Yacht after her. Its name was My Gail 2. Mrs Ronson took to the stage. She stood up proud and confident and delivered her speech with aplomb and flair. I stood towards the back of the room nearly at the front door beside a bike and watched her and the crowd who all seemed to be genuinely taken with her. The applause rang out as she finished and then it was lunch time where fine food and service awaited. Not for me. I think I got a cheese sandwich at someone else's desk.

By about three pm the party was over. All the guests bar a few had gone and as far as I know Gerald Ronson never set foot in the place ever again. The staff relaxed and for the first time there was a sense of team spirit and belonging. People were laughing and telling jokes, the directors wandered around congratulating us and themselves on a job well done. We were in, it was done and the next part of the history of Suzuki GB could start. In fact it had started.

Almost immediately after the event my new office had been decided on and I moved in. It was upstairs along the right hand side of the building about halfway down the corridor. The office was split into three sections with a larger open area for secretaries etc and two smaller individual offices, one of which was mine. It worked fine with me tucked out of the way so I could spend all day on the phone and writing stuff, my new secretary, Debbie, out in the main part.

Some of the media had reported the event but to be honest it wasn't going to make much headline news and so the PR gain from the whole show was deemed to be low level and no one much looked.

It's worth saying at this point that everyone who worked for SGB had been under some serious pressure in the run up to the move south from Croydon to Crawley. From the normal staff member who had to first make a decision to stay with the company, then to adjust to different working hours because of the commute and then the change of scene and inevitable working changes. Then to the more senior managers and directors who had key responsibilities for the move and their own staff. The directors in particular had significant pressure on them over and above normal commercial performance to enable their departments to move in as smoothly as possible so as not to drop the ball or any other part of the puzzle. Some of the directors were of course going to feel pressure on the opening day. Would everything go to plan, could any stupid catastrophe be avoided like dropping a tray of drinks on a key guest or smashing one of the chauffeur driven cars in the car park. I know we were all under pressure. For me I enjoyed the day but felt that stomach churning fear of cocking up something in such a public and career ending way.

After the big day was over there was a massive sense of relief that all had gone so well and no disasters had happened or if they had they were covered up and hidden from the gaze of those present.

As I mentioned above there was some press coverage but more in the way of an announcement of the change of address rather than an OK celebrity juice type of viewpoint. So what unfolded one day a week or so later was so unexpected and so outrageous that those involved, this includes me of course, were shocked senseless.

About a week or so later the media started to reach the bookstands and newsagents. There was nothing much to report except SGB had moved to a new and very shiny headquarters building. What could possibly go wrong?

I had been getting into work very early over the weeks around the changeover to the new building. Early enough for it to have been noticed by the very few people who were there earlier than me. These included PJ Agg, the now very happy and far more relaxed Chairman of the company. PJ and I had always got along just fine. We didn't talk much but when we did he was friendly and supportive. I even think he liked me. In fact I know he did because he told me so some years later.

So there I was at my desk about 8.15am one morning a week or so after the opening event. PJ's car was parked in his normal spot when I arrived. I had hardly got to my desk when the phone on it rang. The reception wasn't open so I knew it had to be an internal call and I knew it could only be one of a very few people.

I answered my phone to hear PJ exploding at the other end of it at me. He was bursting a blood vessel, completely incandescent and fuming at the same time. I have never seen or heard him like this. What's more I wasn't sure what I had done to make him this way. I wasn't at fault, my stomach was wringing and I could feel the blood rushing to my head.

What the fuck had I screwed up? The conversation unfolded something like this:

PJ   shouting at ranting at me. Ian have you seen it? Have you seen it?

Me   No, well I don't know. What? What have I seen?

PJ   Fast Bikes, yes Fast Bikes! Have you fucking seen it?

Me   No I don't think so PJ what's the problem?

PJ   Gerald's going to go fucking apeshit, he will explode. Get here now I have a copy. Come to my office now!

At that point he slammed the phone down hard enough to break it and the desk all in one blow and I started running along the corridor my brain chuntering along thinking about Fast Bikes and what on earth they could have done.

I burst into PJ's executive suite of offices to find no one there in the outer office but could see PJ standing at his desk through the interconnecting door. He was bright red and almost jumping up and down on the spot, fuming and waving a magazine about his head. 'Fucking hell Ian who the fuck do these people think they are. Let me read you what this idiot has said. He's reporting on the opening day and Gail's speech he says **'The opening speech was given by Mrs Gail Ronson who was wearing an haute couture green tent'** Here you read it. What on earth do we do now. Gerald reads all the media on him and he'll go through the roof on this one.'

By now PJ had reached an unseen level of explosiveness. He was waving his hands in the air and cursing Fast Bikes magazine and in particular Colin Schiller the editor/owner who had been at the event, and written the piece. His throbbing vein on his forehead was bigger and more throbbing than I had ever seen before.

'Gerald will call me any minute and he'll be spitting feathers. I'm not taking his call. You'll have to take it and explain to him. You'll have to sort this out and smooth it over with Gerald'.

My response was quick and clear. 'Gerald doesn't talk to people like me Peter. You tell reception that you're not in and if any call comes through from Gerald's office tell them to put it through to me. I'll go back to my office now.

I was shaking with rage and in fear for my job. Ronson would be raging at this very public insult of his wife but there was no way Ronson was going to talk to a pleb like me. He'd never even heard of me let alone knew what I did for the company so I was safe from his fury. But I knew that as soon as PJ had rejected his call Ronson's office would be looking for someone else and that someone was going to be me. I got back in my office, still early and without anyone around, and waited for the inevitable.

A moment or two later PJ called me again saying that Gerald had called him, and his secretary, who by now had arrived at the office, had managed to put him off saying that PJ wasn't in just yet. That meant that my phone would ring very soon indeed.

Sure enough minutes later my phone rang again for what turned out to be a never to forget call from Gerald Ronson's PA. I had spoken to her a few times over the weeks and months prior to the new office switch so she knew exactly who to call.

She was always a softly spoken and calm woman and when she introduced herself she was polite as usual. She started off be confirming I was who she wanted to talk to. Then she said that Mr Ronson had asked her to speak to me because he wasn't able to get hold on Mr Agg to discuss the issue with. My pulse began to quicken. She then said the following:

She   'Have you seen the latest issue of Fast Bikes Ian?'

Me   'Yes I saw it this morning Diane'

She   'Have you read the article about Mrs Ronson?'

Me   'Yes I have'

She   'Mr Ronson is extremely upset about what has been said in this article'

Me   'Yes I can understand his concern and I will have words with the editor later today'

She   'Ian do we advertise with Fast Bikes magazine?'

Me   'Yes we do'

She   'Not anymore. Please withdraw all ads booked with them and do not advertise with them again'

Me   'Yes of course. I'll check with the agency and cancel all ads'

She   'Ian do we lend them Suzuki test bikes?'

Me   'Yes we do'

She   'Not anymore. Mr Ronson wants them removed from any contact with Suzuki from today'

Me   'Yes of course. I'll take care of that myself because I run the test fleet'

She   'You may hear from me again on this matter. Thank you for your help and co-operation Ian. Goodbye'

As soon as the phone went down I sprinted off back to PJ's office to debrief him so he knew exactly what instructions I had been given. He was fine with that and knew he'd dodged Gerald Ronson's fury, though for how long remained to be seen because for sure as eggs are eggs Ronson would want to bend his ear about the matter.

Word on the issue was spreading fast throughout Gatwick Road and I was hauled into Denys' office to explain. I wouldn't say Denys thought the comment was fair and funny but he could see a slightly lighter side to the report than Ronson had, which was fair enough. He smirked as he said 'well you better call Schiller and give him the bad news'.

This was a call I wasn't looking forward to making but I knew if I didn't do it immediately I would get found out someway or another and it would bite me on the arse. So I called Fast Bikes office in London and got put through to Schiller. I had never liked him and it was obvious the feeling was mutual. He had his usual disinterested pompous 'I don't need you' attitude, so though I was nervous about the conversation I was secretly looking forward to telling him where his future laid with SGB. I told him the report had been read by me and PJ and all the directors of Suzuki and Gerald Ronson who was furious about what he had written. Schiller wasn't bothered at that point and didn't really say much at all. I carried on and said that the result was that all advertising from his magazine would be pulled and he could expect written confirmation or a call from our media buyers to say just so. But the real kicker was that Fast Bikes would no longer receive any test bikes from Suzuki GB. At which point he started to get angry, telling me I couldn't do that and it would harm us more than his magazine.

I just told him it was out of my hands and the decision stood. He was flustered and getting angrier by the second claiming this and that and he would get bikes from a dealer and it wouldn't make any difference to him.

The call ended and I went back to see Denys who by now had Tom Waterer, the sales manager with him. They both agreed that no authorised dealer would lend them bikes and that the dealer network would be instructed accordingly.

The problem with Schiller and his whole ethos for Fast Bikes was his arrogance. He genuinely thought his magazine was special, something unique and better than any other magazine currently on sale. I'm sure the team at Bike magazine would beg to differ. The truth was it wasn't. It sold reasonable numbers but the editorial stance was always that what they said was better and more worthy than anything any other mag could say. He was trying to be so cool it just looked silly and tripped him up all day long.

How he thought that saying shitty and insulting things about Gerald Ronson's wife would be acceptable to us and funny to his readers was beyond me. So we dropped him like a stone. I think it took several years before they got anything official from SGB. I had further run ins with Schiller over the following ten years or so. In fact it got so bad with him and me that I thought it might come to blows. He was always angry and aggressive and in the late nineties when I was effectively Marketing Director for Aprilia motorcycles in the UK whilst at the same time running my own ad agency specialising in the motorcycle business, with some pretty sexy brands on board, he became more irrational to deal with. He was on a lifelong ego trip and probably on something else too. I had had some sort of disagreement about ads being run that were not agreed to or something similar and was dealing with his advertising lady, Kirsten, who was a joy to deal with. Things were at a stalemate about payment for ads which I didn't want to pay for. I was at the trade day of the Munich motorcycle show Intermot, and among the hundreds of trade visitors I could see Schiller walking towards me. There wasn't much room to hide or dodge off so I just toughed it out and carried on walking towards him. I really thought this might kick off and to be honest he would probably drop me quite quickly. As we got closer he looked up and saw me. He looked straight through me with the look of death on his face and then just sailed on by.

Chimay 1981 the start. I am standing directly above Barry's back wearing the sunglasses.
Picture kindly reproduced with permission from the owner Stephan Vandeputte.

*Barry and Suzuki GB founder and Chairman Peter Agg at one
of the London motorcycle exhibitions in about 1976.*

*Senior staff and guests at the pool final myself standing
talking to Denys and on his right his wife*

Paul Iddon sitting with girlfriend Weed chatting to me at Donington 1982

*Maurice Knight and PJ Agg flanking the bike after a
successful endurance test on the GT750.*

*The 1982 Suzuki GB team line-up pictured at Donington Park. L-R Mark
Boughton, Paul Iddon, Mick Grant, Roger Marshall and Keith Huewen.*

*Suzuki UK Masters pool champion Ross McInnes and on
the right Denys Rohan SGB Managing Director*

*Simon Buckmaster being interviewed by myself at
Brands Hatch for the BEMSEE newspaper.*

Barry Sheene return to SGB early '83.

Barry Transatlantic races on what became the missing Barry bike. He was sensational on this machine at the Transatlantic but was later disqualified for riding an under sized bike.

The famous TR500 Sheene bike now fully restored by owner Terence Williams.

SUZUKI IN THE UK
THEN AND NOW

It's worth noting how much of a difference the market place is between then and now. The two eras are quite different. The Suzuki GB I was at was of course an independent distributor for the factory and a wholly separate company not in any way owned or influenced by the factory. The relationship was strong, respectful and successful. It had been started and cared for by Peter Agg and Maurice Knight, both of whom, in my view were visionaries of the industry. They both knew the power of a brand and poured stardust on the Suzuki brand with the monumental success of a certain Barry Sheene. People who worked for the company seemed to have a stake in the company. We all seemed to be desperate for the company to win and be successful. We loved bikes and put our heart and soul into making it as good as possible.

The market was more complicated in them days but at the same time it was less complicated if that makes sense. Let me explain. In those days the government was still mucking about with the learner bike laws and maximum bike power output and engine sizes a rider could have before and after passing his/her test. Bikes were a very popular and cheap way of commuting as had been the case for perhaps twenty years by then. There were distinct markets; the commuter bikes for those wishing to get in and out of a town to work cheaply and reliably and then the sports bike market which hadn't quite developed in the way it is today.

Honda were always at the top. They could dominate because they had the name, the bike range and the racing pedigree. Second in the sales and market share department were usually Suzuki at somewhere between 17% and 20%. If we were lucky we might hit 22% now and again but that second spot was a reasonable and sustainable market share. Yamaha always ran us very close and sometimes took our second place laurels but we could pull it back with a new bike, good race weekend or a special offer or two. As the saying used to go 'Win on Sunday, sell on Monday'. Yamaha were never far behind us and we liked it that way. It kept us on our toes. We were always leading and developing niche markets for the changing rider profile. Whereas once upon a time most bikes were sold to lower income males the market changed to sports riders and fun days out or touring in France etc. Suzuki had always led with bikes like the Katana, RE5, the Gixer ranges from 600 to 1100 GSXRs. It was an exciting brand which had found its place in a well matured market.

For a number of reasons which I think reflect the complicated market and ownership at the time, the Heron ownership of Suzuki in Great Britain came to an end somewhere towards the end of the nineties when the factory took back distribution. They sold the Gatwick Road facility and moved into their current location in Milton Keynes. Market share had dropped significantly to embarrassing levels. I see the monthly stats to this day and quite often Suzuki are down in 7th place or lower. It's a shameful way to look at the brand now. So why is this, what are they doing and what could they do? As a lifelong marketing bloke I think I know but it would be no more than opinion because I am not privy to any inside information.

The first and perhaps main reason is that the company completely lost its focus when the factory took it back. It became just a department of the factory where most of the profit per unit was almost certainly made at the factory gate. Thus it didn't seem to matter to the UK boys how they did in terms of units and share. They were just a department, an outpost of Hamamatsu. They lost their pizzazz and flair. The second reason is the bikes. I look at the Suzuki range today and frankly lose the will to live. Certainly there is nothing in the current range I would buy. Remember I am a lifelong Suzuki owner from a GT185 through to GT380 and then the big one the GT750. In more modern times I have owned a Hayabusa which sat alongside my Honda Blackbird and finally a V-Strom 1000. These bikes had flair they led from the front and made your wallet wobble with desire. Not so much these days.

Another massive change in the market and clearly a suspect in the decline in the brand strength in UK was the proliferation and success of other brands in the now crowded market. Back in my day there was no Triumph nor was there Aprilia, MV, Moto Guzzi was a poor relative, Ducati was waiting to explode into racing and into your local dealership. BMW had always been there but was as boring as Volvo back in the day. Then they woke up and brought us things like the GS range which totally dominated and created its own sector in the Adventure market. So there is more competition. How do you overcome competition in a crowded market place? You have to stand out which can be done a number of ways.

The primary way is to design bikes that make people look, bikes that stir the soul and rattle the gates of passion. Bikes that make a rider rush to their dealership to take a peek. Suzuki has for some years lacked flair. They are simply boring bikes. They are not innovating like they did with models like the RE5 and GT750 and remember the Hayabusa which created its own rabid publicity machine concerned only with which bike mag could ride one at over 200mph.

So Suzuki need to wake up and shake up. Get some new designs and make something so full of the X factor that they blow the competition out of the water. In the mean time they have been very clever at marketing to the 50 plus age group who remember Barry, the Golden Years and the nostalgia of those fabulous two stroke racing victories. Their approach has been highly commendable in getting old racing bikes (genuine or not) out and in front of thousands of us who loved that era and just want to feel close to the bikes and the man.

I don't know where Suzuki is going but I do know that I don't like what I see. The company lost its passion, drive and direction when the factory took it back. It's a bit of a wet Sunday now and unless they refresh everything from the bottom up they will suffer as young and disruptive brands come along and make more hay than Suzuki are doing.

They seem to have forgotten, if they ever knew it, that the first rule of advertising and publicity is

GET NOTICED! If you don't get noticed then rules two to ten don't matter...

MAY 1982.
THE NORTH WEST 200.
JOHN NEWBOLD
AND TRAGEDY

This was perhaps one of the defining moments of my career with Suzuki to date. The events that unfolded over the course of the 1982 North West 200 race weekend were unique and shocking. A team member got killed. That team member was John Newbold or as he was affectionately known 'Noddy'. Nothing I say here can make that any easier to bear for those involved and in particular his wife.

Looking back if someone asked me before writing this book the date of that tragic weekend I would have said May 2nd because I had to report back to several directors with a debrief of what had happened the following day and I was sure that day was Monday the 3rd which was a bank holiday. But looking at the reports of the event the race was on the Saturday 15th May so I must have returned to Suzuki at Gatwick Road on the Sunday morning.

It started out as normal for me. A normal race weekend except that of course being that it was Northern Ireland and under siege from the various friendlies of both sides in what was a civil war going on, I had to go over on the Thursday with a bag of goodies in the form of spare parts and stuff. On this occasion I flew from Heathrow and I think SGB were kind enough to get me on the helicopter service from Gatwick to Heathrow. Who knew such a service existed but it did; you see the M25 wasn't yet finished therefore the drive between the two was horrendously slow. The only real alternative was a train up to London then out to Heathrow by train from Paddington. So they started a helicopter service which ran several times a day. I was staggered that the powers that be in SGB felt that I was worth the money for what had to be an expensive ticket, or felt that my time wasn't worth wasting on trains etc. Anyway there I was on the helicopter, a service I used several times that year, to Heathrow and then I swapped over to a regular flight to Belfast.

If memory serves me well on this occasion Big John wasn't my man on the ground though I am fairly certain he was with the team when I got there. On this occasion I rented a small car at the airport and set off north from Belfast for the one hour or so drive up through what has to be said is some wonderful countryside. I also have to say that the troubles were fairly hairy at the time with the IRA not afraid to do the nasty on anyone they didn't like including Londoners and other key targets they felt were worth a punt in the UK mainland. I wouldn't say I was scared but the feeling of running into some bunch of hooded terrorists, from either side, in the back lanes of rural Ulster was never far away.

The North West 200 is held on the streets around Portrush in a long street circuit some call the Triangle. It's about 9 miles long and like all street circuits is very dangerous to those who fall. There are many things from stone walls, to lamp posts and other street furniture that hitting at high speed would be very painful. But I was in high spirits as I arrived in the very pretty town of Portstewart just along from Portrush at the team hotel which was situated right on the seafront. It was a large imposing hotel as I recall and though busy was relatively calm from the point of view of being overrun by fans and the like, trying desperately to get inside the wire to meet their heroes.

I checked in with the team, had a chat with Rex White to see what the news was and if anything needed my attention and then found out they they didn't actually have a room for me. What was worse was that Nigel Everett, Mick Grant's chief mechanic, had kindly offered to let me share his room. What I found out later was that it actually meant sharing a double bed with him! Not nice for either of us but the alternative was sleeping on the floor somewhere or in the team bus. I consoled myself that Nigel was a bit of a ladies' man and would probably be 'partying' somewhere else so it wouldn't really be too bad. The weather was bright and pleasant though with a bit of a breeze running. That first night I had a beer or two with the boys met a couple of local journos for a chat and then went to bed. Sharing with Nigel turned out to be much less of a nightmare than I expected.

The start finish straight at the track runs along the seafront and the paddock is in actual fact a very large municipal park which I think was next to the golf course. The paddock was so large and the distances to be covered by the team were so far that it was unlike any normal race event. Even the TT seems to have a more bijou paddock that the NW200. The upshot was that we each needed a Walkie Talkie just to be able to stay in touch. We had some sort of comms deal or arrangement with Motorola and as such had the use of a large batch of radios all stacked in a charging bay. Rex dished them out and promised blue bloody murder if they were lost or stolen.

The Suzuki GB enclave was made up of the team bus, a Ford Cargo truck and a couple of smaller vehicles. With the awning erected and vehicles parked well we had ourselves a nice little unit in which we could operate without being too bothered by intruders. Friday was practice day and qualifying which all seemed good. We were competitive and expected to do well. Both Mick Grant and John Newbold were happy to be there as far as I could tell and frankly it was all going smoothly. The usual team banter and practical jokes were running as normal with poor old Rex White usually on the receiving end. I was astonished that they took the piss out of Rex the way they did what with him being the team manager but he took it all in good part. I would have expected him to kick back but he never did.

Two main practical jokes were played on Rex this weekend before things became decidedly unfunny of course. The first was that someone got the key to his bedroom while he was out, pulled his top sheet and blanket back and emptied a whole can of shaving foam into his bed just for his further shaving pleasure! I know this because Rex called me down to his room for a chat and a quick meeting on the Friday evening. When I got there he was stripping the bed and trying to clean the place up. I think he eventually got housekeeping to send up a full set of sheets. The second joke was particularly crude and hilarious. For lunch at the circuit we just had sandwiches and crisps etc. Rex had ordered a cheese salad sandwich with mayonnaise. Some jolly japer in the team had intercepted his sandwich before it got to him and inserted a new and fresh condom in between the lettuce and cheese. They told me what was happening and we all focused on Rex as he tucked into his tasty lunch. The problem was that for Rex the first bite also included a condom which then slapped him in the face spattering him in mayonnaise just to make things that little bit worse. It was hilarious as the SLAP! of the condom hit him in the face. Rex, bless him, managed to keep control of himself as he removed the offending article from his face. He then re-arranged his sandwich and cleaned his face before tucking in once again. He was used to this type of behaviour. They once took the rubber end off his walking stick and sawed half an inch off it before replacing the rubber cap and placing it back by his desk.

A strange thing happened in the bar of the hotel shortly after we got back that Friday evening. There was no obvious security at the hotel and yet the often over-zealous racing fans were not much in evidence inside the lobby and lounge/bar area. What I did notice was two blokes in their mid-twenties sitting at the bar having a casual drink. They both had that look of military about them. Not too short a haircut but smart and both were wearing different dark coloured bomber jackets. I watched them for a little while and was certain these blokes were not only military but were carrying pistols inside their jackets. As mentioned before I wasn't aware that we had any formal security arrangements for the team but this was northern Ireland in the troubles so my radar was well and truly on. The whole team and plenty of other riders and team members were in the bar and we were all wearing team clothing. So I decided to go to the bar next to these guys and order a beer. As I stood there I said hello. I realised they were English and definitely not locals. So we started to chat. They asked me what team I was with and who were our riders and that on its own proved they were not into bike racing. My interest was piqued. Very soon afterwards and probably against all the rules of the military they admitted to me they were British army on surveillance and were tasked with keeping an eye on things around the town and race circuit. This was astonishing to me because I couldn't imagine why these two would admit such a thing to a relative stranger. One of them admitted he had done the same duty the previous year and his mate at the time had left his handgun on the bar! I joked and pretended not to believe him and not even believe they were army. At that point one of them pulled his half open jacket aside just enough for me to see a handgun in a shoulder holster. I was stunned. We giggled a bit and then I excused myself with my beer and made off back to our little team group.

Race day was once again a very pleasant dry and bright sunny day. The atmosphere, like many a road race circuit, was electric. There were thousands of fans all along the track side and that coupled with the non-stop commentary and chatter on the PA system made for a great feel about the place. We were in good shape. The team looked good and had high expectations for the day. Shortly after I bumped into Brendan

Quirke, an antipodean who worked as a journalist for I think Motorcycle Weekly, the other offering to MCN. He was a good and funny guy and had caught the same plane as me apparently but we hadn't seen each other until now.

Shortly before the main race in which our guys Mick Grant, John Newbold and I also think Roger Marshall was present too, was due off I noticed a touching moment between Noddy and his wife. The team all except me had left for the pit lane and they just had a quiet moment and a cuddle between them before Noddy went off to do battle. I am not sure why but I was asked to hang around the team camp for a while in case, I think they had forgotten anything. There was chatter on the walkie talkie set up between Rex and one or two others. We had one of the guys placed well out along the track to give us feedback of both rider action and weather, so that was a bit of ongoing which I picked up on my radio.

The tension mounted and the commentary volume ramped up, though for me it was difficult to understand what the hell was being said because when you couple a strong northern Irish accent together with a dodgy PA system there's not much left over. I could hear the revs screaming on the start line and then all hell broke loose as the grid took off with the falling of the flag. The noise of these big four strokes charging away into the distance was something else.

I decided I needed to get down to the track to see some of the action. The race was into lap three or four as I recall, I haven't been able to check exactly on what lap when the accident occurred but I could hear the commentary say there had been a crash out near Juniper Hill and the race was red flagged. All riders would return to the grid. At that point of course, I had no idea who was involved and it never crossed my mind that it would be one of ours. Everything went very quiet. Not much commentary or chatter on the radio. I was about in the middle of the paddock when my radio came to life it was Rex White to me, 'Ian are you receiving me this is Rex'. I immediately acknowledged his call at which point he said John Newbold had gone down but he didn't know how bad it was. He asked me to return to the team camp and stay there for further info.

I wasn't too concerned because there hadn't been anything on the PA system and nothing else was coming in to me so I wandered back to the camp and stood there on my own. It was some time later perhaps 10 minutes or so that Rex cam on the radio to me again. 'Ian this is Rex again where are you exactly?'. 'I am on the back of the Cargo on the tail lift so I can get a better look over towards the start line'. Rex then said 'I'm coming back to see you now. I'm in the middle of the paddock please don't go anywhere'.

I looked out and perhaps three hundred yards away I could see Rex's figure hurriedly walking towards me. He then called me again 'Ian I need to talk to you now come towards me can you I don't want anyone near us'. That was strange because a few minutes earlier the whole paddock and especially around us was empty. But steadily since then a few people had arrived and were milling around. There was suddenly a dark and foreboding gut-wrenching feeling.

As I jumped off the tail lift and walked towards Rex I knew something bad had happened. Rex was just approaching me about twenty feet away and I could see the look of horror in his face. Rex's lily-white skin was whiter than ever. 'Ian it's John.'

Rex stopped for a mini second and then composing himself said those words 'He had a big accident. He's dead'. The shock and impact of those words knocked me off my feet. Nothing can describe the feeling. It was just horrific. I got up visibly shaking and Rex grabbed me by the shoulders and said 'listen the bike will be back here soon I need you to get something to cover it up with so we can get it in the Cargo without any photos being taken of it. Then we will need to sort things out. This is awful Ian. John's dead'.

We both turned around and very smartly got back to the truck. Rex went inside the team awning and I went into the Cargo. To be honest I don't know where it came from but as the little pick up truck arrived with the bike I found myself holding a discarded carpet or blanket. Some of the team mechanics had arrived back by now too and had put two wood planks between to pick up and the Cargo on which to slide what was left of John's bike across. I covered the bike up as best I could and stood on the tail lift to help. By now there was quite a crowd and some photographers were snapping away. I didn't hear any PA announcement yet everyone seemed to know that John had died. The old rubber necking morbid curiosity went into overload with everyone around us so I shouted out 'There's nothing to see here, Please leave us alone, go away'. The bike went inside the Cargo, the tailgate dropped down and was locked and all the team who were there went inside the awning which was then hurriedly zipped up.

I remember there being a complete shocked silence inside the awning. No one said much at all though quite what we could say that would be any good was beyond most of us. Everyone had that ashen faced look of total despair. Some had tears in their eyes others looked at the ground. In a very calm but authoritative way Rex stood in the middle and gave a little speech and some clear orders. He said some nice things about John and that no one here should talk to the press or in fact anyone outside the team about this. It was a public road circuit so different laws apply. Rex was of course talking from experience as just a year or two earlier Tom Herron had died in the same race. He then asked everyone to work together to pack everything up and return to the hotel as soon as possible where we would have an update on the situation. Rex then grabbed me gently and said 'We need to talk privately. I have already spoken to the Police who won't do any paperwork until the coroner has been informed and apparently he's playing golf somewhere! They're finding him now. I need to call the office and tell the directors before this gets on the news and they find out before I can de-brief them. You go back to the hotel now and call Denys and any other directors who need to talk to you. We need to get John's body released asap and off this island'

Rex was an experience race team manager who was quite visibly shaken by John's death but knew there was important stuff to do which wouldn't be helped by either of us falling apart with grief right at that moment. I went straight back to the hotel where I was met by a couple of news reporters at the front door and some sympathetic staff inside who offered me tea or something stronger. I avoided the strong stuff but a pot of tea delivered to my room instantly as I put in a call to Denys Rohan. In the next hour I spoke to Peter Agg, John Turner, Denys again several times and even Edna Calder. They were all deeply shocked and saddened but at the same time were amazingly supportive of me and Rex. They told me to do anything we had to, not to worry about cost. Sort out the paperwork etc and report back to them as often as we needed. John Turner was perhaps the most surprising on the phone to me. John was the corporate toughie a hard businessman who did Ronson's bidding and was never afraid to wade in and hurt your feelings if it was required. But he said something quite deep on the phone to me. He said something along these lines. That Rex and I were on the ground trying to sort out a very difficult situation on different territory in the middle of effectively a civil war. Rules are different there and you need to do whatever it takes to sort this out and get John's body released. He made it clear that Rex and I had full authority to do what was necessary and the board of directors would fully support us. He told me to call every hour or so and gave me the home numbers of all the directors who were waiting for an update from me and Rex all night long if necessary. I remember asking him what we do when and if John's body is released because we only had the team transport with us and there's no way we would be allowed or want to bring John home that way. It was his answer to that one point that made me realise how they wanted this solved. He simply said 'Ian you will need to hire a jet from Belfast airport to remove John back to UK. Get him to any English airport and we'll do the rest then you get yourself back here because Rex will have to take care of the team guys.' Rex arrived shortly after that and we sat in his room and chatted. The hotel had sent up more tea and sandwiches for us as we made more phone calls.

By this time it was perhaps four or five o'clock in the afternoon of the Saturday race day May 15th. All the team were back at the hotel so Rex and I went down for a meeting with them all in I think the back corner of the bar which was for the most part empty anyway. As you might imagine the mood was black. Rex explained that we needed to get the body released and were having a problem with the coroner and Police, but it would be sorted out by morning. John's wife was locked away somewhere in her grief. That we should keep quiet and not talk to the media and that I was tasked with getting the body back to the UK. It was about this time or perhaps a bit later when we were still mainly in the bar that someone came in and said they we had been given permission to go to the hospital mortuary and were able to see John's body. This seemed both unbelievable and macabre to me, but a number of the team wanted to go. They tried persuading me but I remembered my dad's words to me some years before when he told me that one of the things in life you should never want to do is see a dead body, so I declined. They all shuffled out of the hotel and away to the morgue. Not something I regret doing.

As the evening progressed Rex and I went back up to his room to make more phone calls and the hotel kindly shifted me into another room on my own so as to make the calls a little bit more private. Nigel got his room back so we both had a little privacy. By mid evening the coroner had been met by the Police and I think Rex went too and explained the situation. He had promised to release the body with the papers the next morning, Sunday, and we could make arrangements to have John flown home later in the day. So now I had to call John Turner again to update him. Once again John, together with the other directors, was amazingly supportive. He told me my one job now was to find an aircraft suitable to take John and his wife back to UK. He said 'Get a Yellow Pages and find aircraft charter companies and start calling. If you need any help call me'.

So there I was sitting in a hotel room in Northern Ireland with a copy of the Yellow Pages on the bed in front of me flicking through its pages to find the section for plane charter. Strangely as it seemed there was such a section and it was much bigger than I had expected. Hiring jets was not something I had done before so I just dived in and started calling companies based at Heathrow first of all. I called about three or four all of which answered my call which surprised me as well, being that it was now about 8pm on Saturday night. To each one I explained who I was and the difficulty of our situation. They were very sympathetic but no one could help me. It was either not something they did or they had nothing available. But then I found an entry for The London Air Taxi Service. I called and spoke to a really nice guy who took all the details and said he would call around, because as far as he knew there were plenty of cargo planes in Belfast and one would surely be suitable. He asked me about Suzuki GB's ability to pay and said these things were always paid for up front so how would we pay? I had no idea except that between John Turner and Denys Rohan, Heron Suzuki GB would pay. I agreed to fax over to him my business card and the telephone number of the hotel, which I did a few minutes later. I went off to update Rex who was back in his room making more phone calls. We sat in quiet for a few moments just muttering stuff under our breath and cursing what had happened. Then the phone rang, it was the guy from the Air Taxi company. He said he had an offer of a cargo 747 which was en-route to Heathrow the next day but was happy, for the right money to divert to any UK airport with John's body and wife. I quickly accepted but it seemed unlikely that it would really be a 747. He faxed over some contact details and said he would keep on top of things. I had to explain that I would be going to Heathrow first thing and so he should remain in contact with Rex after breakfast in the morning. Rex and I then made a joint phone call to John Turner explaining everything about the plane and payment etc and that I would be back in UK by lunchtime. In this call John made it clear that the whole board wanted to talk to me and that I should come via the office first before going home.

And so with a very heart heart and a monster of a head ache I went to bed to wake the next morning not quite believing what had come about the previous day. There was no time to waste I got up and showered, threw my things in my bag went down for a very quick breakfast and to say good bye to the mechanics and Rex before speeding off back to Belfast airport only to bump into Brendan Quirk, the journalist from MCW, in the queue for the same flight back to London. He was also full of remorse and sadness about what had happened So we checked in and flew back together where he said he would drop me in the centre of London so I could get the Gatwick Express, or whatever it was called back then, to either Gatwick or Three Bridges which was closer and easier for Gatwick Road.

It was Sunday. The office was of course not open for normal business but this was far from normal. My car was parked as usual where I had left it along the side of the building and the directors' parking bay had five or six vehicles in it.

I had a quick chat with the security guard who by now was well aware of what had happened and entered the very quiet and strangely dark building. I knew exactly where to go, the corner office suite and board room where I found some of the directors sitting there waiting for me. It was very calm and slow as we chatted. They each asked specifics of the event and the day from start to finish. I must say once again the directors were amazingly supportive of me and Rex and our efforts. They were ahead of me for the first time all weekend as they now knew that the flight had indeed taken off and landed at East Midlands airport. John's body had been collected by the undertaker for removal to his home town. I felt they wanted a first hand report from me to tell them what they needed to know. It was important to them to feel connected to the events. There was no doubt about it the directors were as deeply shocked and saddened as any of us who were there. It was a sad day and the discussion we were having never got any lighter. We all agreed that nothing can prepare you for a rider's death and this one had really caught us off guard. They thanked me once again and I set off for home.

Instead of sleeping in or taking it a little easier the following morning I was up and in work as early as I had been at any time in recent weeks. As the staff came in they chatted quietly amongst themselves. The feelings of despair and grief were palpable with most conversations being held in hushed tones. I had a steady stream of visitors and had to attend a management meeting for the motorcycle division to update them so they could all replay news out to the dealer network. My telephone also never stopped ringing from friends and media contacts who were reassured to hear it all from the horse's mouth so to speak. Rex and the team were still on the way back and wouldn't get there for some hours yet.

At about the same time as all of this was happening along with the move to the new building the company had bought out or arrived at an arrangement with Graham Beamish for the distribution of Suzuki off road bikes under the Heron Suzuki GB wing. Graham had now arrived in the building proper with his own staff and office. I liked Graham a lot and got on well with him but he did say something odd about the John Newbold death and which I felt was out of character. He could not understand why I was the only 'manager' or director going to the funeral a week or two later. He felt that I really shouldn't be there as he felt I was representing the company and there should be a distance between us. Also he felt that I was looking backwards and we should now be looking forward. That's not to say he didn't have any sympathy for John he had loads but he felt the future was what we should focus on now. I didn't agree at all and along with Rex and the other team members, but noticeably no directors, I went to John's funeral near Somercotes in Derbyshire.

Life does indeed go on and despite the issues of John's death we all had to press ahead. Along with Suzuki off road bikes being with us the new building also had Echo Power products which is a very good brand of Japanese chainsaws and garden machinery. This was run by the two importers, Les Woodcock and Steve who had started the business near Brighton. So, with them and also Bell Helmets we seemed to have a busy and now largely full new building. Not all in the garden was rosy though. Unfortunately there seemed to be a real personality clash between Graham Beamish Suzuki Off

Road boss and Les Woodcock of the Echo power products division. I don't really know why they disliked each other but I can definitely say that Les liked to make silly piss taking comments and Graham was used to running his own show and not taking any shit from someone he held in very low esteem. There was even a whisper that they had almost come to blows at a management meeting with Graham, who was considerably smaller than Les, taking Les gently by the throat and lifting him up the wall! Not sure if that was true but I did get the impression from Graham over lunch one day that he was close to the edge where Les was concerned.

Graham and I had organised an off-road dealer event where the new range of bikes were on show. At this event which we were to hold in a large meeting room/banqueting hall in a local Crawley hotel, he also wanted to launch a much enhanced dealer profit margin promotion which was to rise to 25%. For this he required me and my ad agency to make a massive fake 3D gold bar which he would reveal from behind a curtain, and on it would be the new 25% deal. So I set about arranging everything from hotel booking to dinner and drinks menus to rooms and gift packs to press releases and dealer packs which would contain all new model by model brochures and of course the new 25% offer. In fact we had a hoot with all the salesmen in attendance too. Orders taken on the night would attract the new 25% dealer margin which was, it seemed, a very attractive offer. After the dinner and presentation the sales team were let loose among the assembled dealers with great enthusiasm fuelled by copious amounts of free booze, always a winner. The net result was a bumper order book and a decent hangover to take into the office the following day.

WHAT'S BIGGER, A LOAF OF BREAD OR $100,000 IN CASH?

Just along the road from SGB headquarters is a small right hand turn into a country lane, which felt all the stranger because behind you as you made that turn was a bustling Crawley Industrial Estate and then in an instant everything change back into The Darling Buds of May territory. Not far down the lane is what turned out to be the SGB local boozer called the Greyhound. It was famous for two things; Firstly it was owned and run by what appeared to be two identical twin bothers, and second that it was the venue for the annual world marbles championships. Who knew there was even such a thing as a world marbles championship?

Wikipedia says this **'The British and World Marbles Championship is a marbles knock-out tournament that takes place annually on Good Friday and dates back to 1588. It is held at the Greyhound public house in Tinsley Green, West Sussex. Teams of six players participate to win the title and a silver trophy. Wikipedia'**

A very friendly pub it is too and welcomed us, the Suzuki Bunch with open arms. We would often slip around there after work for a quick one before heading off home. On one particular evening Denys Rohan was there along with a few others from the company. I was downing a pint of foaming real ale when Denys came over to check that I was in the office the following day. He said he might need to me to do something and not to tell anyone about it. Honestly this wasn't that uncommon in SGB so I just took it all in my stride and carried on drinking. But it was in the car home that I thought more about what he had said to me. It was only a short conversation but he said 'You do know Virginio Ferrari don't you?' I reminded him of the meeting with Virginio and the photo shoot at Beddington lane the previous year. All Denys said was something like 'Oh yes of course, well you may need to collect him from the airport tomorrow.'

By the following morning I had forgotten all about the previous night's conversation so when Denys called me mid-morning to pop round to his office I was wondering what this could all be about. I walked in, shut the door and didn't even get the time to sit down when Denys told me he wanted me to drive to Gatwick Airport, meet Virginio and his manager, who I had not met before. Take them to the Hilton for some lunch and then do something very odd indeed. So odd it has never happened to me since. Denys wanted to make it very clear I was, under no circumstances, to bring them to the SGB building. 'Just take them to lunch and go to Lloyds Bank Wimbledon High Street. They are expecting you. At the bank you will collect $100,000 in cash. All three of you will count it and you Ian will sign for it. Put it in this holdall bag thingy and drive them to Heathrow. Get them on the 6pm flight to Geneva and only give them the money when they pass through to departures'.

Denys must have been watching my face contort with surprise and amazement as he told me what to do so he repeated it except this time with a piece of paper with the flight details typed on it. He also made it clear that this was private and must not be discussed or repeated to anyone. At no point did I think the money was illegal payment or anything underhand but I did wonder why on earth $100,000 in cash was being manhandled by me and handed over to Virginio. I nodded to Denys, didn't ask any questions, went back to my office, told my secretary I was going out for the day and I couldn't tell her anything about it.

At this point in my Suzuki career the Ford Fiesta had been replaced I think with a very nice two litre Ghia Capri automatic and I say that because as I drove to Gatwick I said to myself how embarrassing it would have been to collect Virginio Ferrari and his manager in a crappy light blue Fiesta.

Virginio's face shone out from beneath his amazing mop of black curly hair as he and his manager arrived through the sliding door of Gatwick arrivals. They were both very happy and friendly, no big surprise to me as Virginio was always happy and smiley whenever I met him. On this occasion I suspect it wasn't my company that was making him smile. I don't recall them even asking once to visit the new and shiny SGB headquarters. I just told them we were having some lunch and then going to the bank. No one discussed anything about the money. We walked across to the Hilton from the terminal and were met by one of the usual waiting staff who knew me.

The restaurant at the Hilton was a light, modern and airy affair with large windows overlooking parts of the south Terminal.

They both spoke about the race season and the bikes and how happy they both were to be back with Suzuki. To be honest, money aside, it was a very enjoyable get together lunch. I enjoyed their company and guessing by the way they ploughed through their food I would guess they were both hungry. After lunch we headed to the car and I made an excuse that I had never been to Lloyds bank in Wimbledon and couldn't actually remember ever going to Wimbledon. They weren't bothered though as we set off up the M23 and made our way to south west London. It all went quite easily so that before we knew it I was parked in the road just along from the bank.

Black holdall in hand all three of us entered the bank and I asked for the manager by name. 'Who shall I say wants him? Said the receptionist. 'Ian Burgess from Suzuki GB, he's expecting me'. It's at this point when you think that despite this supposedly being top secret everyone else knows what's going on. She seemed to make a secret nod and lifted her eyebrow a little as she acknowledged me and went off to find him. Lloyds bank Wimbledon was one of those old school banks that have largely disappeared these days. It was probably a Victorian building with dark wood panelling everywhere. The manager arrived promptly, shook hands and told us that 'everything is set up in the special meeting room'. Jesus this was like being in some James Bond movie. The Secret Squirrel levels of Secret Squirrelness were rising by the minute. We were led through the secure doors inside the main body of the bank and into a large side office with more dark wood panelling and a very long wooden boardroom type table. In the middle of which was a pile of cash. Dollar cash. Next to it was a book of some form, like a ledger and a sheet of paper with the details of the cash being taken. It also had my name on it and a signature line.

The manager chappie who looked like he couldn't sweat even with a gun to his head, calmly told us what was going to happen. He was impeccably polite and had a slight grin on his face throughout. We were all to count it separately, then tick the box on the paper that we had counted it and verified that there was indeed $100,000 in cash, and then I was to sign for the money on behalf of SGB, except I think this had little to do with SGB and all to do with the grand prix team finances. The money was in blocks of one thousand dollars each with a paper sleeve around it. So we started counting. Carefully and as quick as possible separating the bundles as we went. First it was me and surprise surprise I found there was actually $100,000 sitting on the table in front of me. Then Virginio followed by his manager counted and verified the amount. I signed and they initialled the paperwork. Then came the funny bit as we carefully packed the loaf of bread sized lump of dosh into the black holdall and Virginio's manager tried to take hold of it. I said no and he wouldn't let go. It was all light-hearted but I made it clear he couldn't have it until it was time to go to the departure gate. When we got in the car having thanked the manager at the bank front door I placed the holdall under my legs as I drove to Heathrow.

Heathrow had a bad reputation at that time for theft and pick pocketing so I held on tight to it as we made our way through terminal Three. We had made very good time so were somewhat early for their flight to Geneva or Zurich. The only thing to do was sit and drink coffee and laugh. It was like a stress reliever. Giggling erupted and a feeling of a job well done wafted over the three of us. The problem was they knew the whole story and I didn't and never would. Was it a back hander? Was it bung money from HB Tobacco? Was it anything to do with the team or some other dodgy deal altogether? Actually it was most likely part of his contract payment and he'd asked for it in cash. To be honest I wasn't that curious because I knew if I had the balls to ask Denys he would refuse to answer and dismiss my question in a heart beat. Their flight was called and so we warmly shook hands, giggled even more and said goodbye. At that point the money was handed over and they went off. The next day I told Denys everything was fine and that was it, job done. Nothing more to be said. When I next saw Virginio at a race later in the year we chatted, but he never mentioned anything at all. All in a day's work at Suzuki GB for me. I loved my job but realised that the unexpected is what to expect. Or as Garry Taylor used to say about bike racers 'the only thing predicable is their unpredictability'. And the answer to the question is that $100,000 in hard cash is about the same size as a loaf of bread...

On any given day in the office I would receive letters and phone calls from people trying to blag something for free. Usually it was people riding to the North Pole or the Gobi Desert wanting a free bike and sponsorship. Then there were the photographers, or maybe I should say 'photographers' who would try and twist my arm to lend them a bike or multiple bikes for a photo shoot they were doing for Vogue magazine or GQ or the Times weekend supplement. To be honest they were always nice but rarely did their claim stand any scrutiny. We also had artists and sports stars wanting free this that and the other. The other usually included a free car for a year. They all got turned down. We just didn't have the budget but sometimes a call would come in that was of interest. Sometimes it was a celebrity or their agent. I remember once being at The London Motorcycle Show when it was at either Earl's Court or Olympia. It was press day and early in the morning so though the place was all action with stands being finished off and exhibitor staff running around there were few media at that point. I was on the Suzuki stand doing my thing, which was usually checking all the press packs and give-aways and then doing anything anyone else wanted. This often included polishing bikes and helping unload brochures etc. I didn't see this famous face approaching me and only found out she was there when she tapped me on the shoulder quite hard. I turned around to find myself staring at Pamela Stephenson, she of Not The Nine O'clock news and Billy Connolly fame. At the time she was a big TV star in the UK and not known for any biking connection, so I was a bit surprised to see her there. 'Are you Ian?' she said. 'Yes I am are you Pamela Stephenson?' I said cheekily. 'Well yes I am' came her reply with a massive smile that could light a whole coastline. 'Have you got a minute to chat about bikes?'. And so we chatted away for some time. She wanted some info on various bikes, maybe for Billy if she was even with him at that point, because Mr Connolly was big into bikes. We chatted away for some minutes and then she wandered off to chat up some other PR from Honda or Yamaha. But I have to say she was totally captivating and very pleasant company.

An hour or so later I was approached by a journalist and photographer from Campaign magazine. You almost certainly won't ever have heard of or seen Campaign magazine because it was or was largely London centric and sold out very quickly on publishing day around the book stands of the capital. Campaign was the bible of its day to all and sundry in the advertising, marketing and public relations game. It was about A3 in size and printed on glossy white heavy weight paper. I loved it and eagerly read every page of the whole thing including all the lovely job ads in the back section. My advertising and marketing career, at least the one I thought about in my little head from time to time, included becoming a director of a proper real London advertising agency. If this was to happen at some stage in the future it would probably start with a job found on these very pages. The journalist with his photographer mate were into bikes and wanted to do a short interview with several marketing bods from the bike industry to see what was happening vis a vis bike marketing and agencies etc. I said yes answered a few questions and had my picture taken on the stand. All the while this was going on I could hear the voice of David Farquhar when I first started at SGB telling me that my job was to get Suzuki into the papers and never me into the papers. He finished his little sermon with this advice 'Ian *you* are not the story'. Luckily I doubt if anyone in HQ had ever heard of or read Campaign so a week later when my moment of glory was published I was safe.

On one occasion my phone rang in the office and I found our wonderful receptionist asking if I could ring a chap called Richard Branson. 'It's not that Richard Branson I'm sure' she told me. 'He's rung several times and wants to talk to you about borrowing some bikes. He's got your name and is desperate to talk'. She gave me a telephone number and for a few minutes I pondered about who this guy could be. There's only one way to find out so I dialled the number. Almost immediately it was answered by a bloke with a strangely familiar voice. I introduced myself and he was gushing and really, almost overly friendly to me. He said he was looking to borrow certain bikes for an advertising shoot to do with his shops. By now I was fairly sure it was *THE* Richard Branson but had to be certain so I asked him what his business was. He was a little flustered because he was sure I already knew who he was. In his characteristic semi stutter he said he was in the music and record business. So I said to him 'Oh you're *the* Richard Branson then' to which he just laughed gently and agreed. Once that hurdle was cleared we got along just fine and in fact he was so relaxed I could hardly believe that he had all this time to chat with me a no one. There was no ego or pomposity or assistant or PR department, just him. I made a note of what he was looking for and why and said I would check things and get back to him. He asked me to call asap on this number as it was his direct line. In subsequent chats I found out he was working from his boat moored somewhere in West London. I spoke to Richard a few times and he was always the same calm, relaxed and easy-going chap that he comes over as on the telly. We did indeed lend him a few bikes though I'm not sure what Suzuki got out of it in real terms, but that's the nature of the marketing business; sometimes you spread the love and a bit of product to see what it delivers and stirs up.

On another occasion I got a call from a sponsorship consultant looking for a short term sponsorship deal at a very discounted rate because the original sponsor had pulled out. The call came from a certain Richard Busby who was punting the soon to be televised ITV Pool Masters Championship with top Pool players from the UK and some from the US. Not something we would ordinarily be interested in but he got me interested so we agreed to meet the following day for a general chat with no commitment. The pure coincidence that I would only see about two years later was he was working out of an office in central London, the office was in fact a leading sales promotion agency who would offer me a job in late 1984. It was this job that got me into the agency side of the business and would eventually lead to my being a director of another even larger agency. But I digress a little. Richard was a very convivial chap and convinced me that the deal on offer was extremely good value. It was. The offer was that the two nights of telly coverage would be national on ITV and the whole thing would be called the Suzuki UK Pool Master Championship. The beauty was that the fee of £13,000 was a steal and could be spread across all UK Suzuki brand budgets because we would all benefit. In reality it cost each Suzuki brand about £2000 plus some expenses to get key dealers and guests to London for the event. I wrote a short paper to sell the idea to Denys and he bit at the offer. Because it was sort of last minute we didn't have a great deal of time to publicise it but rather we let ITV do that which they did. They did trailers and promos on the channel in the few weeks prior so all we had to do was deliver the branding and set to the venue. Once again Denys was very easy on me but made sure I knew that I need not fuck this up live on television.

In fact it went like a dream. It really wasn't much work for me or Richard's team as the UK Pool organisation were in charge of the event and the ITV producer and director were completely relaxed. On the Saturday evening when the final was being played we had probably forty odd staff and dealers in the posh end of the audience, Suzuki got masses of brand exposure and Denys presented the trophies. My role apart from publicity and setting the deal up and getting it in motion was to organise the players from our perspective and make sure what would be seen on TV was exactly right. That included me running the vacuum around the television set! It was a great event with little Ross McInnes from Scotland being crowned champion.

As per normal the week was for normal PR work and the weekends were for racing. It seemed I was always away at weekends at one track or another, bring another car load of bits on the Friday evening and in another hotel. But I loved it. The team was doing well with the home team of Huewen, Grant, Marshall. Iddon and Boughton all getting stuck into the various championships we were contesting. The riders were all very slick and professional. Some like Mick Grant had been at this a long time and knew how to behave in public, not that Mick was a handful out of the public eye. Others though, like Mark Boughton, were not so accustomed to being in a higher profile team, getting the eye from all and sundry at all times. He was a good-looking lad with a mop of dark hair and a big smile from his very white teeth. I got to know Mark a bit during this season. He did ask me a very odd question at one point. He was dating a real stunner called Anita. They made a good looking couple but he wasn't sure if being in a solid relationship was good PR for his image as a young and rising star. He genuinely asked me if I could advise him if it would be better for them to split up and he be promoted as a jack-the-lad man about town. I have to say that stopped me dead in my tracks. Image advice is part of the job if they had a terrible image or were racing in threadbare leathers etc but relationship advice? I steered well clear of that one. Him and Anita stayed together as far as I know for years after he stopped racing. Sadly Mark was killed riding a road bike in Ibiza, Spain in 2001. He was riding one morning, came onto a slip road to find standing traffic and hit the back of the last car in the queue. He was only 41.

John Travolta anyone? Well almost but not quite. In spring 1982 I received a call from Ammes Gardner who was marketing manager for Lee Cooper jeans in the UK. He was very excited in a laid back sort of way to tell me that Lee Cooper had teamed up with the distributors of the new Grease movie, Grease 2, which was coming out later that summer. Would we, Suzuki, be interested in reaching a youth audience by joining them in a big promotion throughout the summer which would involve massive exposure in cinemas, and also in Woolworth stores across the country? I knew little about the new film and assumed it would star John Travolta again but sadly not. It did star Max Caulfield and Michelle Pfeiffer, so not all bad then. Ammes and I agreed to have a chat at the Lee Cooper head office in Essex and then go and see the film distribution company in London's west end. Ammes was a very pleasant and laid back kind of guy. He knew his stuff and was easy to get along with. It was clear there were plenty of connections between the film, his product and the youth audience for Suzuki. So a few days later I hopped on a bike and sped into central London to meet the film people with Ammes. They too were highly switched on to their audience and were determined to make as much noise about this film as they could. We quickly reached a proposed deal where we would supply a few GS125 bikes to win in a nationwide competition which would be promoted by leaflets, ads and Woolworth instore and cinema in-lobby point of sale and promotional displays. There was a real energy about this film mainly due to the original Grease being such a phenomenon just four years prior. Sadly quite a bit of that energy was lost when Woolworth got involved as not only did they have one of the dullest marketing men ever but Woolworth being such a huge concern made them as slow as molasses where decisions were required. However, Ammes and me persisted and got it done. The result was you couldn't move in bike dealers, cinemas and Woolworth stores up and down the country for promotional blurb and bikes on show promoting the film and the competition. It was a good deal for us too because apart from a bike or two to give away it was relatively cheap publicity. Plus I somehow became friends with the film distribution company who very kindly put me on their 'guest' list for film premieres and private viewings and pre launch screenings. I would get a call or a little invitation in the post asking me if I would like to come and see a new movie. There was a massive pre-launch screening of ET for example which I went to and was dined and well looked after afterwards. But for Grease 2, yes we all now know it wasn't great, but the publicity for it was enormous and we all benefitted from it. There was even a Grease 2 promotional party at Stringfellows nightclub in London which I went to. Wow what a night that was. Famous faces everywhere most of whom I recognised but couldn't remember their names so kept well clear. I even had a chat with Peter Stringfellow himself who was nothing like I was expecting. He was such a genuine and nice man who seemed pleased to have met me and those at the launch party. Nice guy.

The remainder of the 1982 racing season, at least for the SGB team was reasonably successful but not outstanding. I remember poor old Mark Boughton having great rides but no real results. In fact though I couldn't find the results data for the season I do remember something about Mark not finishing any races or at least it seemed like he hardly finished a race. I also remember there being an issue with his mechanic not providing let's say a full service approach to Mark's race bike prep. I don't remember there being an issue between the two of them personally so maybe the mechanic had other problems that he brought to the track and workshop.

Of course the big issue for the racing community was Barry's mega crash in free practice at Silverstone for the British Grand Prix. He was flat out on track and hit the already downed bike of a 250 or 350 rider. The track marshalls had failed to flag the accident and Barry hit the bike at tremendous speed causing crushing injuries to his legs and many other parts. Barry had been on title winning form throughout the season and was likely or at least fully in the hunt to win a third world title. The accident was a massive blow to everyone, no matter what team or manufacturer you worked for. Likewise the whole race fan community around the world was horrified. Barry was very close to winning a third title and even if he came in second place he would have almost certainly carried on with Yamaha for the 1983 season. What most people don't know is the accident caused a massive legal issue because there was a liability claim against the track for not having a marshall at that point or if he was there not doing the flag waving which indirectly caused Barry's huge crash. Obviously I don't know all the facts or even a few of the facts but I heard a year or so later that Barry received a £2,000,000 payout from the insurance company. That has never been confirmed or even talked about publicly but it makes sense if you add up Barry's lost title hopes, the injuries and the knock on effect of not competing £2m seems reasonable. I'm sure Barry would have wanted to not have the accident, that almost goes without saying but the cash would have eased things slightly in the future for him and Stephanie.

Late in 1982 I was surprised and a little hurt to be informed by Denys that I was to get a new boss. Denys had decided that the company needed a more general marketing manager and had appointed Ian Catford who had been at both BMW and Honda in years gone by. To say I was hurt and offended would be an understatement. I had given my all to Suzuki GB, had done it for slightly less than fuck all pay, plus I was cheap to run on expenses etc. I had shown both my worth in the job and brought many a good deal and excellent results in my areas of responsibility. I totally accept that I was at times stretched too thin and could do with more help but to just bring in Mr Catford was wrong. At least it felt that way to me. Now once I had met Ian Catford I was a little less angry because he seemed reasonable and made it clear he didn't want to cut across my existing job responsibilities but if I am honest I could smell a rat. He was clearly going to build his own team and was playing politics. By that I mean I just had a hunch about the man and it wasn't good. Given that I had few options, loved my job and the people at SGB I wasn't going to spit my dummy out but immediately Catford was there I noticed that my access to directors and influence in meetings and planning were being cut away. I could see there would be trouble when in a casual chat with Ian about his experience and what he wanted for SGB he simply and coldly said 'I'm here for the duration'. That to me said that I wasn't there for the long term and he was going to be trouble. And that's exactly how it turned out but not for another six months or so. The one thing Ian Catford knew very little about was racing so he kept well away from me on that. He also hated getting his hands dirty so running the test bike fleet and dealing with the media were areas he left well alone to me. He was pleasant enough in a snake in the grass kind of way or at least that's how I looked at him. I am probably judging him unkindly because over the years following my departure I met Ian and he was always kind and friendly but that's maybe because he got his way. At the risk of getting side-tracked a couple of years after leaving Suzuki my old boss John Norman, who had been head of the car department in my time at SGB and subsequently had been elevated to group chief executive called me out of the blue one day at my ad agency job in London. I immediately hoped he wanted me to take on some SGB advertising or sales promotion work but not at all. He wanted me to meet with him and Ian Catford to discuss an 'opportunity'. I said yes and then

Ian Catford called me to sort out the meeting arrangements. It was kind of odd because he wanted just to have a lunch with me and John Norman at a Crawley hotel but he insisted I came to the SGB headquarters in Crawley first. On the day I got to the building and of course immediately ran into any number of old colleagues and work mates. It was like a re-union just for me. I was wandering around the building with my hosts shaking hands and feeling very happy to be back in the family. Except I wasn't there quite yet. I even had a couple of chats with old colleagues who asked me about stuff as if I was still PR manager and still employed. It was if I had never left the company.

All three of us went off to an hotel outside Crawley and had a casual lunch where they grilled me on my current job, the bike market, and how I would feel about coming back should that be an option. They didn't quite commit to anything but said that Ian Catford was about to re-organise the marketing function of the whole company and could do with someone like me back in the fold. I was almost flattered but it was obvious they weren't about to offer me a position. They left it hanging. And hang it did. I never heard another thing from either of them. Thanks chaps. John Norman did the same thing again in 1994 but more on that later.

JANUARY 1983, THE RETURN OF THE PRODIGAL SON

Barry Sheene. I was a fan. Brands Hatch 1974, not sure what event but me and my mates on a bunch of FSIEs and assorted other mopeds zoomed off the twenty miles or so from Bexley to Brands Hatch to join what was a massive crowd to watch an International or British Championship round. We loved it, the atmosphere, the revving two stroke engines, the smell of Castrol R, the cheering but most of all Barry, who it must be said we didn't know too much about at that time. As his star rose so did the fandom and the adulation. Literally tens of thousands of fans would cram into every corner and every viewpoint of every circuit where he raced. They lapped it up, he lapped it up. He was unbeatable, had rock star looks and a Glam Rock lifestyle. Every inch of news and every detail of his life from his wardrobe contents to his cars and famous number plate was analysed to within an inch of its life. He told us to Splash It All Over and he had probably, for me anyway, the sexiest girlfriend on planet earth. The Stephanie and The

Barry were perfect for each other. The media loved them. Non motorcycle media too. The cross-over of Barry from bike racer to popular hero known by millions in the country was complete.

I first spoke to Barry at Silverstone in I think 1975, in the outer paddock area as he arrived with Steph on race day. His Roller drew up and the crowds parted like the Dead Sea as he parked by the entrance to the inner compound of the paddock. I was lucky enough to be right there standing next to him as he got out of the car and I blurted out some nonsense about my cousin Graham working for SGB. The noise of fans cheering and shouting his name out was enough to wake the dead but to my surprise Barry heard me, said he knew Graham and wished me all the best. I stood there for maybe half an hour hoping he would come back, which he didn't but at that moment I knew I wanted to be inside the wire. On the best side of that paddock fence. At that point I had no plan and little idea of what being on the inside would look like or how to go about it but as this book has shown things can and do conspire to let you achieve your dreams.

And now I was about to find out that Barry, The Prodigal Son, was returning to ride for Suzuki once more in the 1983 season. Not only that but I would be involved and apparently Barry was very happy about that.

So back to January 1983 at SGB headquarters, Gatwick Road, Crawley. A normal day for me. Nothing much to report and not expecting any bad news or explosions. It was deep winter and cold outside, not biking weather at all. The phone rang and it was Denys. All very normal, we spoke a lot during a typical week. 'Ian have you got a minute I need to talk to you about something'. No problem I'll be right along I told him. I told my secretary I was just going to see Denys and wouldn't be long, then I casually strolled along the upper corridor towards the front of the building turned right to where the directors' offices all faced out over the front lawn and entrance area of SGB. Deny's office was third or fourth along. He was sitting alone at his desk. I knocked, he called me in and told me to shut the door. Nothing unusual in that either, so I wasn't expecting anything but a quick update meeting on the usual day to day flow of PR and marketing services work. I don't think I sat down. Denys then looked up from his papers and said something like 'You know Barry Sheene don't you Ian. I mean you know him' the emphasis was on the word *know*. 'He says he knows you quite well' Denys continued. It still hadn't dropped that what Denys was saying was that he had been talking to Barry and that I came up, however slightly, in the conversation. 'Ian I am going to tell you something now that is top secret. So secret that very few people know about it. You must not tell anyone about it outside this office. Anything you say must come through this office. Do you understand? Don't respond to any questions or speculation inside or outside this building'. My heart rate slightly rose but I was totally unprepared for what Denys said next.

'It's bombshell stuff and I need to trust you'. I was probably just nodding my head and looking confused or perplexed as Denys then followed all that preamble up with this little corker, **'Barry is coming back to ride for Suzuki this season'.** I think Denys had to tell me twice because as I recall the room went very quiet in my little head when I heard these words. I was stunned and shocked. I said nothing at that point. What should have happened next was an in depth discussion about what he had just said and the why, and the back ground to this momentous announcement. But it didn't happen because I just stood there while Denys started on the details of what would happen next and what my role would be.

'Secrecy is everything at this moment. The launch of Barry's return to Suzuki will be next week at Donington Park. You will organise and take care of the whole event. I will not be there and neither will any other directors. Only you and Rex will be there plus a small team crew and the bikes plus of course Barry. Barry is going to call you tonight to talk it all through, oh and the **Daily Mail has been given the world wide exclusive on this'.** At that point reality kicked back in and I got on board properly by telling Denys that he cannot give a world wide exclusive to just one media outlet. It would be counter productive and in fact work against us and Barry. Other news papers would be really annoyed. 'It's just too big a story Denys. You'll piss off all the other papers and they simply won't cover it. You'll get one day's coverage in the Mail and nothing in any of the papers except if you're lucky a one-inch newsflash'. I know I wanted to ask who the fuck came up with such a stupid fucking idea of giving it only to the Mail. But didn't in case it was Denys' idea. Denys argued for his Mail exclusive but I convinced him to trust me and my knowledge of how this works. To be fair on Denys he was man enough there and then to change his mind in my favour and allow me to organise the whole event including who would be invited, which would actually be the world's media pack. Denys politely told me 'not to fuck it up then'. He carried on and then finished the meeting with this 'you need to write a basic launch announcement release for the media which we can fax and telex out to all concerned in the next day or two, but in the meantime call Barry and talk it through and between you both come up with a plan for the day'. I had to ask Denys who knew at this point so I could discuss it privately with them if required. Basically it was the board of director, Rex White, me and Ian Catford. But he made it clear that other than talking to Rex privately I should say nothing to anyone. 'It must remain secret for as long as we can keep a lid on it'.

I walked slowly back along the corridors of power in a state of shock but massive excitement. I passed a couple of senior managers and just said hi. They looked at me in an expectant sort of way as if they knew about it but I think everyone I looked at over the next few days would have that look about them. The reality was as Denys had said, very few people knew. I don't even think Ian Catford said anything to me about the deal and certainly he didn't get involved at all with the Donington launch. All afternoon I had to try and carry on as normal whilst in my mind writing various press releases and thinking of how to arrange the day. I couldn't and didn't tell my secretary until the last moment a couple of days later. The one person I absolutely needed to talk this through with before talking to Barry was Rex White. So I went down to the race work shop to find that it was largely empty of bikes and staff which was nothing unusual at this time of the year. The new bikes wouldn't arrive until February and people were busy doing other stuff. In actual fact what was happening was Rex had organised one of last year's bikes to be sprayed up differently in a new colour scheme but not with Barry's famous number 7 or his name on. Rex was sitting at his desk when I walked in and immediately shot me a friendly but don't say anything kind of look. It wasn't difficult for Rex to talk in a hushed whisper kind of way because that's how he always talked. 'You've spoken to Denys I hear'. 'Yes just now'. 'Well it's you and me and we need to talk but not here'. 'Barry's calling me tonight so how about we talk after that' I said. 'OK I'll call you later tonight'. And that was it. A nudge and a wink between us and few words.

As I climbed the stairs back up to my office Deny's secretary was waiting for me on the halfway landing area, she whispered 'Denys has spoken to Barry and agreed that it will be your plan to have a full-on media launch day at Donington next week. Date to be confirmed tomorrow'.

Now, my normal routine for a regular evening in my tiny one-bed flat in Peacehaven was to do not a lot. I would eat something uninteresting, watch something uninteresting on the tv and maybe struggle into bed about 10pm. Fall flat out asleep and then start the new day bright and early for the trip back up the M23 to Crawley. I had bought the flat with the much needed help of one of the local building societies with something like a 95% mortgage on 15% interest. The flat was brand new, light and bright and suited me ideally because I was never much in it. It took zero maintenance and would cost me almost nothing in heating as it was quite well insulated. I didn't even have enough money to fully furnish it. The interest rates were crippling in the early eighties. If I was lucky I had enough money for a pint or two at the Telscombe Tavern on a Sunday night. But I loved it. The place was mine and I felt sort of grown up. On this particular evening nothing was going to be normal and uninteresting, far from it. I grabbed something to eat and waited for Barry's call. Denys must have given him my number. Barry had had my parents' number for a few years now but I had never given him this one. I was super excited an almost hyperventilating while waiting for the phone to ring. When it did ring I nearly jumped out of my skin. Pen and note pad ready I picked it up. It was Barry. 'Hey Ian it's Barry. How are you?' It was strangely very odd to have Barry calling me. My hero. My bashed and broken hero. We chatted like old friends. He was really stoked to be coming back to SGB, the place where it all began as far as he was concerned. I asked him questions about his fitness and general health - he ignored them. So I changed tack and asked him about why Suzuki and why did he leave Yamaha. Once again he sort of ignored those things. He was sure he would tackle those questions on the day and I shouldn't worry about them or get involved. It was clear at Donington he would do all the talking, he would tackle the detail and he did not want to waste time on the past. What was absolutely clear was that he was really looking forward to working with me and getting stuck in after the press day. He then asked me what I was doing tomorrow. Obviously I told him I would be writing a teaser press statement for all the media outlets and press associations and talking things through with Rex and Denys. 'Well when you've done that and you have more details about the Donington launch why don't you come round here for a chat. 'I'll call you in the morning' he said. To which I was sort of shocked in my answer 'You can't call the office Barry, no one knows and I'm sworn to secrecy'. 'Don't worry ace I'll get Steph to call then she'll hand the phone over to me when you answer'. With that the chat was over. My heart rate had settled but not much and immediately the phone rang again. It was Rex. This call was simple. I copied Rex in on everything I had said and agreed with Barry, he then told me the circuit had been booked for the following Thursday which gave us nine days to get it all arranged. We agreed to chat again in the office and that was it. Cloak and dagger finished for one night at least.

The next day was to all intents and purposes a regular day in the office. No one knew anything much and I said nothing to anyone except Denys and Rex when we met for a short chat later in the morning. Rex said one bike was ready, it was a runner and we could if we wanted get Barry to do some demo laps. The hotel had been booked and I told them that I was about to go and see Barry to go through some of the details. That was it, all very calm. We agreed that the next day a basic and intriguing press release would be sent out to every known newspaper and association asking them to come to Doningtom Park the following Thursday for an announcement of mega proportions. Apparently the Daily Mail had been stood down as the paper of exclusivity on the basis that the story was already leaking and they couldn't get exclusivity no matter what we did. It wasn't leaking yet but would do in a day or two.

I went back to my office to get a call from the front reception desk that there was a Stephanie on the line for me... I said yes put her through and found Barry on the phone almost panting with excitement. 'Ian you haven't been here before have you? But you know where I live don't you?'. 'Well no Barry I don't actually.' I sort of knew the address, The Manor

House, Charlwood village and knew that I could get there via the airport inner security road, which wasn't secure at all. But I didn't know how to get to his actual house. So Barry told me where the entrance was and asked if I was free to come round there and then. He did it in his usual inimitable way 'are you busy?' he said. Well no Barry I am not busy apart from running the entire PR and marketing service operation for the whole company oh and planning your *Return To Suzuki* event for the following week I am completely free and frankly bored to death. Actually I was as excited as he was to be asked around to his house and have a chat about what was happening in a week's time. In fact Denys probably knew that Barry was going to ask me there and had I not gone he wouldn't have been amused. But I jest there was no way I was turning down the chance to visit Barry's house. So, still in a veil of secrecy, I slipped out of the office and drove the ten minute ride to Charlwood. In fact Barry's house was very easy to find. I was really nervous about driving up to the house along their gravel entrance track. It was as though I had crossed a secret threshold by being invited to this place. You have no doubt seen pictures of the house from the many taken of it and then in and around it over the years of their ownership. But nevertheless it was fairly impressive. A Tudor or Elizabethan house of some age but I am not sure how old it really was. I parked out front, grabbed my briefcase and walked up to the front door. I pulled the handle for the bell or rang the bell, can't remember which it was and very quickly Stephanie came to the door. She welcomed me with a 'shoes off' shout as well as a 'hi Ian come in, tea or coffee?'. I followed her to the right and into the large kitchen where she chatted away as she made the tea. Barry was on the phone in his office she told me but would be along very soon. Now I have to make it clear here that I always thought Steph was lovely. She was never less than chatty and very friendly to me, as long as you took your shoes off at the front door everything was fine with Steph. Next thing I knew Barry was walking along the narrow, carpeted corridor from his office into the kitchen. He was his usual self, all smiles, handshakes and welcomes. 'Grab your tea and let's go into my office'. He was off, walking away as I said thanks to Steph and quickly rushed after him.

Barry's office was exactly as I had seen it in many photos. He sat in his leather Chesterfield sofa with a small coffee table thing in front of him which his famous Mickey Mouse telephone dominated. In fact the MM telephone was massive, much bigger than I had expected. Barry just sat there and kept smiling. He didn't say much immediately but when he did he said something like 'well then, what do you make of all this then?'. I was sort of in dreamland being there in his house, in his office and talking to him about the launch event of Barry's return to Suzuki, but at the same time I had to focus and get real. Because it was real and we had stuff to plan and agree. A few minutes later it was just like having a meeting with anyone else in the office. I told Barry what I wanted to get from the day for publicity purposes and he told me that he wanted to do all the press briefing etc. I told him I would have some live radio interviews lined up on the phone and he told me he wanted to get out on track and do some parade laps. He also told me that we would be talking a lot and that I should always leave a message on his answerphone because he had it on loud-speaker, and only picked up when the caller had identified themself. It was really enjoyable to be able to just sit there, just the two of us and chit chat about his return to Suzuki. I had always got along with Barry and it seemed he was quite happy that I was handling the day. Inevitably I had to get back to the office and he had calls to return. What we did agree on was that it would stay secret until some days' time and that we would talk every morning between now and the launch day at Donington.

Back at the office I met Denys again and debriefed him on my meeting with Barry. We also discussed the list of media outlets and press associations we needed to contact and I asked how we would announce this to the staff and if Barry would be coming in to the office for a walk round or staff launch. Denys rather strangely said that Barry would not be coming into the office. I got the impression that there was an issue or a problem between them about this. Maybe Denys had asked and Barry had refused. I decided to keep well clear of that on but did ask him how we would announce it internally. It was decided that there would no fanfare or big shout-out but just to let the news spread around naturally over the next few days. My next job was to call some of the bike press and tease an announcement and the launch of something big at Donington the following week. I also called a contact of mine at London's Capital Radio and another at Reuters News Agency.

The following day my phone was getting pretty active. People were beginning to put two and two together and arrive at the answer – Barry Sheene! I don't really know how they could know this unless we had a mole because I wasn't saying a thing and the list of those who knew was very very short. I got several calls from the bike press begging me to give them a scoop but it just wasn't possible or worth it. Sure they were doing their jobs but I needed to keep mine and despite being called probably five times a day by MCN I said very little except that it was big news and all would be revealed on the day or perhaps the day before. My main message was that they didn't want to miss this for anything.

Two days before the event we sent out a more detailed press statement that Barry was indeed returning to Suzuki, the home of his two world titles in 1976 and 1977 and that we would welcome the media at Donington Park circuit to meet him and the team the following Thursday. This message was sent out by fax and telex and if my phone was hot in the days running up to this announcement it was positively nuclear in the hours afterwards! It simply did not stop ringing. I got calls from all over the world, even Japan from one of the television stations who very politely requested permission to send a tv crew to Donington. A request I was very happy to grant.

Internally within Suzuki GB when the news was announced there was a massive collective smile and excitement buzzing through the whole place. The only downside was that everyone knew Barry lived ten minutes away and could not understand why we weren't getting him in to have a meet and greet. My answer was the same to everyone that there's not enough time this week and he'll pop in soon. It seemed to work but to be honest I thought it a big missed opportunity.

The next few days just flew by. Every morning about the same time Barry would call me or vice versa and I would update him on what I had done and who I had spoken to. Likewise Barry knew hundreds of journalists and tv celebs etc and he had been working the phone hard too. It was quite clear to me given the calls from national and international papers that we would be inundated on the day, so I briefed Barry that it would be full on all day. He was really excited but it was nothing new to him. He'd won two world championships with all the attendant press intrusion and coverage. He was calm in a very excited sort of way.

The day before the launch event the team left SGB early with bikes and some basic team equipment to make it look like a proper garage for a GP and I followed them up a few hours later with all the press packs, launch pics and my lists of names, telephone numbers and contact book.

I drove up with my stomach turning with excitement. It had been decided to stay at the hotel where Barry and Steph always stayed for Donington Park, the Donington Manor Hotel. I had never been there before because the SGB team always stayed one junction further up the motorway at a large group hotel. But I have to say it was a good choice being how close it was to the circuit and also more intimate. At this time of year I don't think they had many other bookings if any. So when we and the media bunch all booked in it was like a second Christmas for them The place was heaving when I arrived about 6pm. Journalists everywhere, our team led by Rex White. As soon as I walked in I was pounced on by numerous journos all wanting exclusive one to one interviews with Barry, that night. Not a chance I told them. Nothing gets revealed until 10am the next day at the circuit. No favours, no specials, no sneaky peaks. Even journos who couldn't get a room at this hotel had come in to try and get an exclusive with Barry, but Barry was tucked away in his and Steph's favourite suite where they always stayed and wouldn't be on show until they came down to dinner and even then not for interviews. I sorted my things out in the room and then went down for dinner which we all agreed would be together as one unit so as to block out unwanted guests and journalists. I entered the small dining room and was pleasantly surprised to see that it was pretty much full of SGB staff, plus Barry's own team mechanics and Barry, Steph and his parents tucked away in the far corner. Barry just looked up at me and winked with that cheeky little grin he always had. They had decided to put me at the end of the main table more towards the dining room entrance door so that I would be able to chat to and intercept any stray journalists who were making a B line for Barry. Actually over dinner it seemed to be fairly quiet but as soon as I finished and stood up so did Barry and Steph. I didn't see Barry's parents go but they disappeared and left me and Barry in the lounge area inside the entrance reception area of the hotel. He wanted to run over the final details of the next morning so we found a quiet corner and hunkered down on a sofa. That was the start of it by us sitting there in public Barry had become available and easy prey for the media. I was batting them away quite politely but they kept coming. The difficult one for me was the sports writer for the Daily Mail. He and his paper had lost a world exclusive and though he was superficially polite, and knew he had to get a story, he was more than a little peeved. He was pushing quite hard for a one to one interview there and then which I firmly declined but I did promise him one for the following morning. I felt sorry for the guy because he was staring at defeat really by virtue of the number of journos from all over the world who had descended on that little corner of Derbyshire or is it Leicestershire? I never did work that one out. As the Daily Mail guy was about to leave I thanked him very much for coming and said how much I looked forward to seeing him again in the morning. At last Barry and I were alone for a moment. But what happened next I really didn't see coming. He turned to me and quite angrily said 'never say thanks to the press. Just don't do it. You never thank the press'. His teeth were gritted and he was quite upset with me. I was shocked that he could think that way given how many thousands of pages he had received over the years and that he felt he could tell me what to do. I just replied from my gut by saying 'you don't have to say thanks Barry because you're Barry Sheene, but *I do* have to say thanks, it's my job'. Barry calmed down immediately and moved the conversation to something equally unexpected.

'You do press ups Ian don't you? You're fit and always going to the gym etc. But can you do one arm press ups?' Of course I said yes and the challenge was made. Barry was certain he could do more one arm press ups that me and so right there and then in the lobby lounge of the hotel I was forced to show my one arm press up ability to Barry. Now, normal press ups were a thing of mine. I could rattle off up to seventy in one go but one arm jobbies are a different thing altogether. So I tried by assuming the normal two arm press up position and then moving one foot much wider out to balance against the removal of one arm. It worked a bit but after four or five I was falling all over the place. Barry swatted me out of the way so he could do his thing. It was obviously his party piece and I knew I was about to be beaten, and in public. He got down but sideways to the floor, not face down. He was on one arm and started bobbing up and down with ease. They were indeed one arm press ups and I was indeed humiliated and beaten. He must have done twenty or so. To be honest I think this was a well thought through way to prove to the media that he was fit again after his horrendous accident six months previously at Silverstone. We both knew the question would come up from the media the next day. With smiles and laughter all round and much appreciation from the few who were watching we called it a night.

Bright and early the following morning we all met up again for a quick breakfast. I had been outside with Rex White to check the weather which was dreadful. It had snowed over night and was laying everywhere in a dusty covering. It was also bitterly cold and windy. Bloody terrible. Once more I was surprised that no directors of SGB had come to the event. It seemed astonishing to me that such a special day could be totally avoided by those who were paying Barry's enormous fee for riding. I have no idea how much SGB were paying him but Barry was well known for getting incredible deals and vast sums for his services. To put this into context Denys once let it slip to me that he had agreed a $600,000 deal for Randy Mamola for the 1982 season. Randy was a great rider but with no world titles to his name and with a manager, Jim Doyle, to pay too but that was probably a small fraction of what Barry was receiving. So why weren't they there? In the week or so before the Donington launch it was agreed that Rex and I would be the only 'managers' in attendance and that was justified with the position that it would allow Barry to be centre stage and no off piste questions would be asked because no directors would be in attendance. But for me it just seemed like they didn't care. I'm sure they did care but...

We set off for the short drive to the circuit from the hotel in a decent size convoy. At the paddock gates; high and metal sheet large affairs, we were allowed in and then they were shut and locked tight. Even at that early time a full hour before we would open them for the press they, the media, were massed at the gate. TV crews, vans, photographers on ladders propped against the fence so they could train their long lenses on the scene inside. The interest was amazing and it grew as the minutes clicked by. The sky was that blue grey affair with a flat cloud base that only winter gives. It had the look of more snow and the wind blew steadily and very cold across the circuit. We had taken over the large scrutineers' garage at the end of the pit lane. It was just a bare concrete floored tin roofed affair and with no heating at all we knew we were in for a day. The garage was, I would say, about fifty feet wide by sixty or more feet long and with large doors at both ends. In the far corner by the pit lane was a wall-mounted telephone which I had arranged with the circuit bosses to have available to us for the whole day. It was on this phone that I would tee-up the radio and other non broadcast interviews with Capital Radio and other news journos who couldn't get there on the day. Capital Radio wanted a live to air interview with Barry so it was essential that I had my timing agreed and could drag Barry away when the slot became available.

The massed media at the paddock gates were beginning to get very fractious with the cold and the wait so shortly ahead of schedule we opened the gates. What happened was totally astonishing. They literally ran en masse across the gravel of the paddock to get to the garage and to Barry. My best guess is that we had a total of between fifty and sixty journalists scrambling to be first in front of Barry. We never had any order to it and no chance to make a statement to them as a unit about Suzuki's intentions for the season with Barry.

I remember a very polite Japanese television crew bowing and asking me in broken English please for an interview with the great Mr Sheene. No problem at all, it was soon set up and they went for it. Barry was wearing a new and very nice dark brown leather casual jacket from Dainese. It had a sheepskin trimmed collar. Frankly he looked great in it but it didn't have the Suzuki logo anywhere on it. So in a rare quiet moment I asked Barry to swap it for a Suzuki team jacket just for ten minutes. That's when I saw the irritable side of Barry once again. He snapped at me 'I don't wear Suzuki jackets or any other clothing except for my race leathers. I'm not doing it Ian so don't ask!'. He quickly followed this up with 'I never miss a chance to say Suzuki and always do the best job for Suzuki. They'll know who I ride for!'. With that I stepped back and let Barry's undoubtable media management take over. He was supreme at it and totally in his element. Photographers had Barry on and off the bike, in and out of his leathers, with and without Stephanie. Every which way. I even made sure the Daily Mail guy got his ten minutes' worth exclusively with Barry.

The weather stayed the same so it was completely impossible to get Barry out on the track but we did move the show out into the pit lane for photographers to get more race type pictures of Barry and bike. We also managed to get the cafeteria opened up and hot teas and coffees served for all and sundry. I think we even managed to get some donuts and bacon butties rustled up.

As per usual I had my Suzuki GB camera bag with me, I never went anywhere without it and during the morning took quite a few more relaxed and candid shots of Barry and Steph. Then I had my brainwave. I knew we needed some of our own shots of the day to put together a group of photos that could be used after the event for media who hadn't been to the day or had arrived late to the story. That's when the one arm press up from the previous night in the hotel lobby came to mind. In a quieter moment when some of the press corps had disappeared off back to their offices and to meet filing deadlines I had a chat with Barry. I mentioned that I had an idea for an icon picture from the day and that it was based on the one arm press up. The idea was to get Barry doing one of these press ups in front of his bike and with Steph looking on while standing behind the bike. He loved it, his face lit up. And so it was. We set the shot up and I got down to ground level so as to be at Barry's level. I snapped off several frames all in black and white and left it at that. Little did I know how well used and famous it would become. I use it on my facebook home page and it regularly pops up on the internet to this day. I'm not a photographer but I am proud of that shot and the thought behind it.

By a little after lunchtime the media had everything they wanted and apart from a couple of telephone interviews still outstanding we were done. Rex White and the boys packed the kit and bikes away and left the track. Barry's parents went off with Barry's crew and so in that cold vast cavern of a garage were left me Barry and Stephanie. What he did next will stay with me forever. It showed his wonderful caring and appreciative side which was, I am sad to say, always in conflict and contrast to his irritable and precious side.

Barry came over to me and gave me a huge hug, so much so I thought he'd never let go. 'That was amazing Ian. Press from all over the world and every major newspaper in Britain. TV and radio. Live interviews on the radio. Amazing. Thank you. Thank you so much'. I must admit I was welling up and truly knocked out by his gesture. Stephanie too came over and thanked me. She didn't hug me though which was a massive disappointment! But it didn't end there...

With a huge smile on his face Barry said 'We have the track and my 500 Merc. Hop in and let's have some fun'. With that we all bundled in his grey 500 Mercedes, which I think had the 4BSR plate on it. Me in the back behind Barry and Steph in the front passenger seat. He revved it up and let rip down the pit lane. Out onto the track empty of humans except for us but covered in crispy ice and light dusty snow. He charged into Redgate with the back spinning up a little then down the hill into the lowest part of the track. We were screaming, shouting and hollering as he lost it coming up the hill. Sideways with the back hanging over the rumble strips. Words cannot describe the fun we had as he threw this massive car around and let the ice rip us from side to side. We were screaming and laughing so loud it hurt. Down the back straight and through the little chicane onto the start finish straight for another lap of never in a straight line hooliganery. Finally we crept back into the pit entrance and came to a halt at the garage entrance. An experience I will never forget. Anything else that day was a let down so we just called it a day. They sped off and I tidied the admin up with the track management and left for a long drive into the winter darkness down the M1 to Sussex. The die was set, Barry was now officially and publicly back at home with Suzuki.

Bright and early the next morning I was back in the office reading all the papers which were full of coverage. I debriefed Denys and other key directors on the day, Rex came and joined in the meeting and I must say there was a sense of job well done and a very satisfied glow about the place. Many staff still didn't know what was planned and so as that news filtered through the building I had a steady stream of people coming to my office to confirm that Barry was indeed really actually back with SGB. We got phone call after call from Suzuki dealers up and down the country and many of the Suzuki Distributors around the world made contact to join in the celebration. Finally and perhaps the most importantly the factory in Japan sent their congratulations and approval. I sent all my film off by courier to Lab One, who did all our film processing, for urgent attention. The very next morning it was all back with a selection of 10x8 prints including the one arm press up moment. A selection was sent around the directors' offices and another set was approved for use for media. Strangely I hadn't heard from Barry since Donington. That didn't last long though as he called mid-morning asking if I had got back ok and did I have any photos from the day. As soon as I said I had them all back he was chomping at the bit 'come round now then, let's see all of them'. So I packed up everything on my desk and trotted off once more to Sheene Towers. Stephanie greeted me with a smile and a 'shoes off' order. Barry dragged me into his office where we pored over every single pic in either large format prints or on what are called contact sheets which are A4 sheets of small thumbnail shots. His office was covered in newspapers all showing the Donington day. His phone almost never stopped ringing. He was buzzing with it all. I suppose an hour went by with us talking it all through and then he stood up and told me we're off to the workshop. Barry's mum and dad Iris and Frank lived there too. They had their own quarters which was a small cottage attached to the right hand end of the Manor House as you looked at it. As we walked past it she came out all smiles, as was always the case with Iris, and had a quick chat. The work shop was round the back of the building and was much bigger than I had expected except it was old and hardly the sparkling emporium of technical ability you might have thought. Ken Fletcher and Frank were in there beavering away on the bikes. Barry and I had a good wander around and then I had to get back to the office with a list of the pictures Barry wanted for his own use.

JUST AMAZING OR WAS IT JUST APPALLING?

About a week or two later the sales team for the bike division had organised a dealer conference at one of the big hotels at Heathrow airport. It was still a few days away but all involved were flat out getting the bikes, the launch materials and ads together to show to up to 300 dealer staff who would come down to see the whole 1983 Suzuki bike range. What they didn't know was that Barry would make a surprise guest appearance. The idea with these one day national dealer sales meetings is that everyone gets there for coffee and biscuits at about 10am. This is followed by a sales presentation led by Tom Waterer, the sales manager, and then after more details on marketing strategies and pricing etc they can see all the bikes in the flesh. Having got everyone juiced up a little there follows a buffet lunch and a general get together which allows the sales guys to get among them and take a, hopefully, massive order. Financial stocking plans are offered too which means the dealer can order stock and not have to pay for anything for several months.

A couple of days before the Heathrow sales meeting I attended a sales and marketing meeting in Denys Rohan's office. It was fairly straightforward stuff whereby we discussed the timings and who was doing what and the like. No issues to worry about. Most of the guys were to stay in the hotel the night before so as to meet and greet those dealers who were flying down from Manchester and above. Thankfully I wasn't asked to do this and so my role would be dealer marketing packs and materials, which were pretty much all prepared. Denys made it clear to all gathered at the meeting that Barry would be in attendance after lunch but it was to remain a secret. Anyone telling dealers in advance would be in hot water! Denys then told me that I was in charge of Barry that afternoon and that he wanted to talk to me about it later or the next morning. OK then. I wasn't aware that anything I was doing would involve Barry, except that we had some pictures in the dealer pack of Barry in Suzuki leathers for their own local advertising. I think Barry called me at home that night. He was as usual very friendly and chatted away about odds and sods before asking me if I was going to the Heathrow dealer meet. Once I said yes he said 'Great Ian can you give me a lift to Terminal 1 afterwards please because I have to get the late afternoon flight to Leeds and I'm leaving my car at the hotel?'. Of course I would be happy to take him but I asked him why Leeds? It was because he had signed up to make a series of kids programmes for Yorkshire Television with Jan Ravens and Kenny Lynch. The series was called Just Amazing and they would record four or five episodes per day for several days. What's more I heard, though not from Barry, that he was being paid £8000 per episode!

I arrived at the Heathrow hotel just before lunch having had another quick telephone chat with Barry the night before to confirm times and flight details. All the senior sales and marketing team were there including the great Maurice Knight. We were in a very large ballroom which was accessed via big and wide double wooden doors and then down just a few steps to the ballroom floor. At the far end was the buffet area with plenty of round dining tables. To the right was the stage with a projection screen and lectern and all around the rest of the room were probably twenty to thirty bikes. In amongst all of this were two hundred plus dealer principals and sales managers. Actually they loved this kind of event because it got them away from the shop and into conversations with all their mates in the trade. They could swap sales ideas and general chit chat and updates about the business. I had already met Barry outside in the lobby as arranged, he was going to have a bite to eat and a sit down in a side room especially arranged for him so as to keep the secret from the dealers. In the ballroom after lunch the on-stage topic turned to marketing, promotions and the racing activity. That inevitably led to one name Barry Sheene. Not sure who made the racing presentation. It might have been Maurice Knight or even Rex White but that was my queue. The gathered masses were all watching the stage and not looking at the entrance door. I had collected Barry and walked back in through the double doors as the on-stage bit was focusing on the racing activity and the return of Barry to Suzuki. We both waited at the top of the stairs looking down at the mass of dealers in the room. There was no announcement from the stage but the speaker stopped talking and just looked across to me and Barry. I stepped back out of the way, because it was absolutely not about me, and people started to turn around. A few, then a few dozen and very quickly everyone in that room was looking up at Barry standing there. An audible rumble swept through the crowd, then a few people started to clap which immediately turned into a cheer of excitement and total approval. The star was back. The King is dead, long live the King! Job done.

For the next hour or two Barry mingled with everyone, gave of his time and happily shook hands, had photos taken of him and engaged in the small talk of Champions. He loved it and they loved him. The wives and girlfriends in the crowd all gave him a kiss and a cuddle. He was supreme at this kind of thing too. This is what the X-factor really is. It's not just the wins on the track it's that innate ability to be special yet approachable. That rare entity of star quality that makes a huge difference. Everyone in that room met Barry, spoke with him and he made them all feel special. You cannot just buy that special something and Barry had it by the truck load. This proved why Barry was worth the big bucks and how to best use him to your commercial advantage. Let's not forget we were there to sell bikes and motivate dealers and Barry's input was worth its weight in Gold. Barry was aware of his value in such a situation in a genuine and honest way and yes he was brilliant at saying just the right thing to everyone. Of course there were some dealers he had met before and knew quite well but everyone that room was in awe of the man. His charm and charisma made him what he was. He was special.

I was lingering around never far from Barry. We had agreed that I would keep an eye on the time and if he had had enough or wanted a break for ten minutes or so he would look at me and nod or wink. Time had rushed by and all that meeting and greeting was hard work. The little smile muscles in his face must have been on overtime by now. He looked over to me and I knew that it was time to leave. I had arranged with one of the sales team that when Barry was ready to leave I would give a sign to him on the stage and he would make an announcement that Barry has to leave us shortly so if they wanted a photo or autograph please do it right now. That announcement was made which allowed us five or ten minutes to finish up before working our way back through the room towards the door. The sense of elation was palpable in the room as we made it back up the steps to the doors. Barry turned and waved before we exited the room, grabbed his overnight bag and walked the short distance down into the underground car park to find my company Ford Capri. I was a little bit embarrassed about the car because I expected Barry wanted something more upmarket and also because would anyone really like to drive a world champion? But not a bit of it. Barry didn't mention anything except how well the event had gone. He explained more on the drive to the terminal buildings that he was cramming about 8 episodes of Just Amazing in over the next couple of days. Heathrow is massive, for those who have never been there, and driving from an airport hotel to the terminals involves various ring roads full of service vehicles and buses and then the tunnel before arriving at the approach road to the three main terminals. I pulled up to the drop off point outside Terminal One and we got out. Barry was in a very good mood. Happy and cheerful. We shook hands and as always he thanked me before wandering off inside.

Immediately he was approached by several people wanting an autograph or handshake.

In 1983 the first GP of the season was the South Africa round at Kyalami and I was desperate to go. Firstly because I could see Barry doing well, second because I had and still have never been to that part of the world. So in a naïve fashion I asked Denys if I could go as part of the team and get us plenty of extra media coverage because of the Barry situation. The simple answer was a firm and not very polite 'No'. My protestations were to no avail, there was simply no way SGB would fund my costs. So I went back a little later and asked him if I could borrow about £600 from Suzuki as a pay day type loan thingy. That was met with laughter and an equally curt answer, 'No'. That was it, out of options, rebuffed and somewhat bruised. I had one more trick up my sleeve and that was to ask Barry if he could drop it into general conversation with Denys asap. He was happy to ask Denys but doubted it would get me anywhere. He was right. I didn't go. It didn't turn out too well for Barry either as he finished way down in tenth place and over a minute off the lead time of Freddie Spencer.

The second race of the season was an altogether different affair for my attendance in as much as it was the French GP and Le Mans. I was expected to go to this race as we had Keith Huewen riding for SGB and of course Barry. In the week or so before the race Barry called me a couple of times to see if I was definitely going, which I was. He was always looking for a bit of an angle, something extra to focus on, so he proposed a race back to UK! His plan was simple once we had both ascertained that we were driving. I was going down with Keith and his girlfriend and we had already worked out the best and most efficient way to get back to UK was leave immediately after the 500 race. Barry was driving down with Steph and had the same return plan. So that was it. When we each got home, me just east of Brighton and him of course to Charlwood, we would call the other one and leave a message.

I think Keith and I left on the Wednesday in his 2.8 litre Ford Capri which was a bit of an animal. Getting across the channel was the most relaxed part about it from the moment we hit French soil he was on it. It's actually a lot further than it seems from Calais down to Le Mans about 450kms to be sort of precise. The team were already there and well set up by the time we got there which was after dark. Keith decided that instead of just hitting the hotel and a quick dinner before we would go to the circuit to check on things. Getting in was no problem because we had all the passes but when we got to the Suzuki GB spot something lit Keith's fuse. I hadn't heard before of any issue between Keith and his mechanic Paul Boulton but as I was wandering around the camp suddenly I heard shouting and arguing between them. I went back to the team truck to find Keith and Paul really screaming at each other. Keith was issuing orders and Paul was disagreeing. It looked likely this could get ugly so I tried to calm things down a little between them by insisting we left for the hotel. Nothing more was said in my ear shot and I never got to the bottom of it. There was a race to attend to, not trying to sort out what was in all likelihood a silly misunderstanding.

For this event we had decided to give Keith a little bit of a media makeover by having a new Huewen media pack and letterhead designed and for me to see if I could get some more European media interest in the boy. Keith was on fine form and really looking forward to this race. His bike was fast and very reliable, to be honest as it turned out a better bike than Barry had. The first full day, after we got there and the previous night's argument with Keith and Paul, was good weather. I strolled about and saw the HB team Suzuki with boss Roberto Gallina and had a brief chat with Randy. I also checked out Barry's camp which was as professional and well presented as ever. We had a chat about this and that and he gently reminded me of our bet but added in that loser buys the champagne! It was at this point that I did check with him that he hadn't arrived in his helicopter. He said no but it was only when Steph assured me that they had driven that I accepted the bet, again.

If you have never been to a GP or MotoGP at Le Mans take the time, make the effort because it has a certain magic about it. Vast crowds and cheering that sems as though it can be heard all around the circuit make it something very special. The problem for this year's event was it was marred in tragedy.

This from wikipedia *This race was remembered for two fatal accidents that occurred over the weekend in the 500cc class. The first occurred during Friday practice when Italian rider Loris Reggiani collided with Japanese rider Iwao Ishikawa. Ishikawa died shortly after from severe injuries. In the race itself, defending winner Michel Frutschi crashed heavily and was taken to hospital, but later died.*

As for us Keith had an excellent race and result. He kept his head down and out of trouble for the whole nine yards and finished in a truly epic fifth place. Barry was happy with his result or at least put a brave face on it but to be honest finishing in 7th place wasn't what he really wanted or what we had expected. The size of the task facing him was becoming apparent. The bike was low on power and short on upgrades and trick parts from the factory. However no sooner than the race formalities were over and done with we were piled into the car and out of the circuit. No mean feat at a major race but somehow the paddock exit was clear so we made good our escape charging out through town and onto the autoroute heading north east for Calais. Keith didn't let up and before we knew it after a pit stop or two we were on the boat with no sign of Barry and Steph anywhere. In Dover I bailed out and into my own car left up a side street just off the sea front for the last hour or two back to my little flat in Peacehaven. It was late, very late when I got in, perhaps 1am but I still called Barry's home number to see if he was back. The phone rang, as it always did, then the answerphone message kicked in. Nothing unusual here because Barry always did that before picking up if he wanted to talk having heard your voice. But this time he didn't pick up. I left a message claiming victory and said I'd be back in the office on the Tuesday as today (Monday) was Easter Monday bank holiday.

I didn't hear back from Barry during that sleepy and calm Monday and trotted into the office bright and breezy on the Tuesday morning. Everything was as per normal except that I found out pretty sharpish that there had been a mass redundancy of about 22 staff while I was away. It seems the down turn in sales coupled with or because of the government's new learner bike rules had triggered this. I was trying to find out who had gone and any more details about the situation when I got the call from Denys to come to his office. Off I went to give him a full debrief on the weekend. Denys had recently moved in a new corner office more befitting of his position. Personally I thought he had about the best office in the whole building. But when I got there I found him and my immediate boss Ian Catford sitting there with very long faces. I was invited to sit down with them at the meeting table and was calmly told that my position was being made redundant. A brown envelope was slid across the table to me. They thanked me very much for my service, sympathised with me and started to go through my options and what was best to do immediately. I was to clear my desk, say a few good byes and then leave the building. Just at this most inopportune moment Barry charged into the office all smiles and Mr Cheerful. He slapped me on the back, announced I had won the Le Mans challenge and started talking to Denys about the weekend.

'**Not now Barry**' Denys said cutting right across Barry. Barry stopped, took stock of the vista and I think realised what had just happened. He said he'd wait outside for me and left the office. I was pretty much done and devastated. There wasn't much to say at that point so I stood up, collected the brown envelope form the table and left. Barry was indeed waiting outside for me. He asked what had happened and so I told him I was sacked, finished and had to go now. We walked back along the top floor corridor and bumped into Maurice Knight who obviously knew what had just taken place. He was not amused and clearly didn't agree with the situation. Maurice most kindly told me to keep the car, the petrol card and my company credit card for the time being. 'I'll call you when we need them back but they'll help you in the short term'. He was indeed a true gent.

By now I was floating and feeling sick. I was done, over and out, booted out from the job I loved and the job I had given everything to. What's more I was good at it and had made a difference. I cleared what was mine from my office, which wasn't much, and left. Said a few goodbyes on the way out including the guys on the security gate and drove home in a daze. Later that evening Barry called to sympathise. He told me to call around the other manufacturers and the teams I knew to see if they had anything and to get my CV into some London head-hunters. He tried to cheer me up a bit and then said to keep in touch and hung up. That was it, my time in the fast lane had ended up in the gutter.

Over the next few weeks I did get in touch with other manufacturers but to no avail. Things were tight in the motorcycle industry. Garry Taylor the Suzuki GP team boss by then who was by now in charge of the HB team and all the cash that went with it ($800,000 a year by all accounts) asked me to help him with a few projects like new sponsorship and then offered me a job handling the team motorhome and hospitality at all European GPs. I accepted the former and turned down the latter. I needed a real job and fast. We did in fact make a quick dash to Paris together to see the European Chairman of Lee Cooper jeans who was interested in Grand Prix sponsorship. It came to nothing though. My CV was doing the rounds in several recruitment agencies and one morning I received a call from one of these chaps who was recruiting for a middle east advertising agency. Could I come in to see him in his Mayfair office? I was intrigued and jumped on a train to London the next day. There were two of them tasked with recruiting some middle to senior management in advertising and PR who had specific, the guy I had chatted to on the phone and the Managing Director of the ad agency based in Dubai. We chatted, they laid out the job and all the many benefits which of course included a tax free salary well in excess of double that which I got from Suzuki. Plus I would enjoy free accommodation in a two bedroom apartment and a car and health care. What could possible be at fault with this offer? The answer was of course nothing at all except I had no real idea what life would be like, if I would be trapped there and under some sort of contract, which bound me to them for a year or more and generally I wanted to resist it, so I did. Probably a mistake if I am honest. I was under pressure and so started taking any work I could get including delivering Land Rovers to construction sites all over the country. It paid well but was hardly a good use of my skills. I then got a call from the two guys who had tempted me and Suzuki to sponsor the Pool Championship a year or so before. They had somehow heard I was available and needed someone short term to help them through a busy period. They had moved out of the office I met them in before and into a bright little space around the corner. But for meetings and good impressions they had agreed with the MD of the company whose building I had met them in before to use their meeting room. It was on one of these meetings that I had met the MD and started chatting with him. It was quite clear this agency was top drawer with clients like British Airways and Philips. He asked about my background and when I told him I had just left Suzuki etc his ears pricked up. He took my home telephone number and promised to call me that night.

He did indeed call to outline a job they were recruiting for as Account Manager of the Peugeot car advertising business they held. He asked me to come to the office the following day which I did, where I met him and the agency Chairman. We talked for a time, they sold me the task and offered me the job on the spot. I would be paid £18,000 a year, get a brand new Peugeot 205GTi and quite a few other benefits. That was it, I accepted on the spot and so my advertising agency career was begun. I loved it there. The agency was called Salesdesk and was part of the Grandfield Rork Collins empire. This job kickstarted a whole new element to my marketing career which was to last some 24 years! I went from this Salesdesk job three years later to another good but somewhat dull agency and then into the big league with Newton and Godin in Tunbridge Wells which was owned by the huge Grey Communications Group. They were bit players with a world wide annual turnover of just $3 billion! It was with N&G that I achieved my goal of being a board director. A milestone and a recognition of a little bit of talent and a whole lot of luck. For a period we even had the Yamaha UK account but for some reason I was kept well away from it!

SEX, LIES AND VIDEOTAPE

In this final chapter I am going to tell all and explore some of the darker areas of the grand prix racing scene at least as was then. I cannot be certain of everything in this chapter but for the most part I have experienced what I discuss first-hand or it has come to me directly from trusted sources close to the person or event. These sources are always people I knew well and have no reason to lie. In some cases I have heard the same things from two unconnected people. I don't seek to create a bad image of Barry, far from it, but in my position I was able to see and experience elements of the sport and people within it that you might find interesting and which might just add something to your overall understanding of it.

Let's start with Barry being the greatest of all time or as it is usually displayed G.O.A.T. This is a fairly easy one to shed some light on. He wasn't. By any technical measure of performance and wins Barry was successful but not exceptional. He won two world titles and in doing so did it in much shorter season lengths than we have now and won with fewer wins than most champions today would require. Any number of champions were more successful than Barry. Here's just a short list of riders who won far more than Barry; Geoff Duke who won six world championships and six TT titles, Phil Read won eight world titles across four classes, 125, 250, 500 and 750. Also he won eight IOM TT race wins, 121 Grand Prix podiums and more 250cc world titles than any other rider. How about Mike the Bike Hailwood a man who was incredibly popular in the public mind in his career. Or Valentino Rossi with nine world titles to his name and 115 race wins. Or Giacomo Agostini who won an incredible fifteen world titles and one hundred and twenty two race wins. Truly astonishing by any standard in any era. Kenny Roberts, Kork Ballington and Freddie Spencer were all far more successful than our Barry. The list would go on for some distance too if I wanted to push home the point, but I think you get my drift. Riders of course can only race who they are up against on any given day or season. But the point is well made, I think, that Barry was never the greatest of all time. If I had to choose one rider from the above list who could reasonably wear that crown it would be either Giacomo Agostini or Valentino Rossi, but again very different eras with hugely different machinery and outside influences.

So just how good was Barry, why was he so popular and why does that magic remain to this day? In many things in life success is all about timing. Barry was a very likeable and media friendly guy. He spoke well and was good looking. He had sex appeal and at the time of his ascendancy the media were ready for a hero. It was about the same time as James Hunt and of course when the sponsors started to arrive, such as Brut, it broadened the appeal to the general public. It made people realise that motorcycling was not only a practical and cost-effective means of transport but as the new breed of superbikes came along, it was also a leisure and fun past-time. Barry's popularity was helped, and I cannot overstate this, by his relationship with Stephanie. When they did that famous nude photo shoot with her wearing his leathers it was meat and two veg for the tabloid papers to get on board with Barry. At the same time or shortly thereafter he had the Daytona crash which was filmed as part of a documentary. That, though very painful, was front page news and his recovery was followed once again by the main-stream Fleet Street press. All of this helped cement him and his name into the general consciousness. How good was he? Well he won two 500cc World titles and for some years was almost unbeatable. He was daring and dashing and cheeky and very photogenic. Nothing could go wrong it would seem. Even when he left Suzuki in the late eighties and went to Yamaha he was still seen as a world championship contender and boy did he nearly do it in 1982. He touched the heart strings of a whole generation of fans born in the late fifties and sixties who were in their twenties and thirties when he was riding high, and it is those fans who still worship Barry Sheene to this day. How popular was he? Very. I wouldn't be writing this book if he was a forgotten bit-part player.

I'll come back to Barry shortly but I wanted to cover off a few other issues about bikes and racing to show a different and largely unheard of part of the Grand Prix scene of old and perhaps it still goes on to this day. The first point I would illustrate is the issue of the bikes you might have seen around the country at shows and events. These bikes, and I am focusing on Barry's bikes here but I think it could be across the board, are always shown as the real thing, Barry's winning bikes from 1976 and 1977. In reality if these bikes have come from Australia and have been verified by Stephanie I wouldn't doubt them but I have seen far too many of these bikes to accept that they are what is claimed of them. In other words I believe that some of these bikes never raced, were perhaps built after the event or even made up of spare parts. More on that point in a moment. In the 1976 season according to Merv Wright, Team Suzuki Manager as quoted in Battersby's book Team Suzuki page 125 –

'Somehow or other, Barry was able to commandeer all three of the new machines. One as his main bike, one as a spare and the other became known as his 'international' bike.' He went on to say that these were the bikes they had for the whole season. So where are these bikes now? Well as far as I know Barry had one, one went back to the factory, which is normal practice for all factories with World Championship winning bikes and I believe from what someone once told me, that Peter Agg, Chairman of Suzuki GB had the third for his private collection. I have not been able to confirm this. So you then need to ask yourself how many times have you seen in person or in photos someone claiming to have or able to exhibit a Sheene title winning bike? Too many that's how many. There have been I think 'replicas' shown to the public and the public have been ever so slightly conned in the process.

A few years ago on the Barry Sheene legend page on facebook I showed a picture of Barry on his Suzuki T500. I had had that photo for probably thirty years or more and it was signed by Barry. I was contacted by a chap in London who wanted to know a little bit more about the photo and the bike in it. I couldn't help him too much but we spoke a few times and he told me he had that very bike in bits in boxes and he was in the process of rebuilding it. I put him in touch with my cousin Graham Saunders, who had helped build the very machine for Barry and they verified that the engine mods and other parts of the frame etc were the real deal. The frame was the famous Seeley one that had been bought by the Sheenes. Little by little the bike and the story came together. The real bike emerged from the boxes and was totally restored to how it should look. A mighty fine bike it is too and Terence Williams, who owns it and who did the hard miles of restoration, should not only be congratulated but celebrated for bring it back to life. It appears that this bike of Barry's was the bike he competed on most and won more races on than any other bike in Barry's career. It's worth a pretty penny now too. Tens of thousands I would guess. So how does this fit into the issue I am trying to explain here? Well for some years another bike was doing the rounds at exhibitions and sitting alongside other claimed Barry 'originals' claiming to be this very bike. It wasn't and I think it has now disappeared from view.

I can also show from personal experience how this phenomenon works. I saw with my own eyes over a period of months two world title winning factory works bikes in a workshop in Kent. Officially these bikes didn't exist as they had been sent back to the factory in Japan. They were now sitting in the factory's museum as proud proof of a long and successful racing pedigree and heritage. Except they weren't. They were privately tucked away and I saw them many times.

I asked the 'owner' what these bikes were and expected him to fob me off. But he didn't, he just came straight out with it saying they were two factory works bikes from 19XX which won the titles. They looked very genuine to me with scrapes and wear and tear and stickers which were correct but aged well. So on another visit I asked him why he had them and he again gave me a straight answer. These bikes were genuine, would be lightly restored, and then likely be sold into a private collection. So, once more I asked how this could be so when the factory would have wanted these back at the end of the season. He giggled at this point and explained that copies of the real machines were made throughout the season from spare parts and run on practice days to get some engine time on them. They were the bikes which were sent back to the factory but the real bikes were in his possession. I heard that this was not uncommon practice during the mid to late seventies. The two bikes I saw were indeed sold into a private collection, the proceeds of which helped fund a villa in France or Spain.

Barry had two issues in his life, in my opinion, which were his downfall. The first and obviously most tragic problem was that of smoking. He smoked regularly from an early age, some say about the age of eight or ten. He always seemed to have a fag on the go and one only needs to spend a short while looking at photos of him to see that he rarely didn't have one lit up. I had mentioned it to him at one point, not to have a go or try to tell him what to do, but to get him to understand that it was bad news. He once told me that it was better now because instead of smoking the uber strong agricultural Gitanes untipped he had switched to Marlboro. Still bad news in my opinion but he assured me it was better for him and that he had cut down on the amount he smoked too. I have no idea if that was true but I noticed one day when he returned to Suzuki that he was ripping the filter off the Marlboros which he said was because it made them taste better! I do know that in 1988 at the British GP at Donington he wasn't smoking. I was there with my wife and our first-born son who was just four months old. We had been lucky enough to get paddock passes and were pushing the baby buggy around when we bumped into Barry. It was like old times. Barry was as always super friendly and made plenty of time to have a good chin wag and catch up. I noticed he wasn't smoking and he probably realised that I had noticed and chipped in very energetically and proudly that he'd kicked the habit. But it wasn't to last. According to my Australia correspondent Barry was back at it over there. The smoking eventually did for him and very sad that is too. To those who justify it by saying he crammed into his life more than ten other normal people would I say so what. He still died way too young at 52 and would have gone on to greater things. It's like saying to someone who's mum had just died at the age of 89 that she'd had a good innings or a good run. Yeah but she's my mum and she's still dead!

There was another second issue that Barry had problems with and that I have alluded through this book. If you like your hero Barry Sheene squeaky clean, the best and unbeatable on every level you may wish to look away now. Barry had a sex issue and it nearly undid him a number of times. In the years of television stars being outed and accused by girls of unwanted attention and worse I often thought of Barry. I am not saying he raped anyone, far from it but sex was a problem for Barry and there's no sweetening the pill except to say it was a different world back in the seventies, and it was. I've never been a pop star, sports star or famous even for a day so have never had the pleasure of fending off eager young girls. But Barry was very famous and certainly had plenty of female admirers and plenty of offers no doubt. The problem with Barry was that he just couldn't say no or remain faithful to Stephanie. I saw it myself at the Brands Hatch test day when I turned up with Nina my Sun Page Three girl. Barry was out and out trying to pull her not twenty feet from Stephanie. As I found out some months later he had indeed pulled her. On the inside of the paddock fence so to speak it was common knowledge that Barry would shag anything that would allow him to. Ok it was a different world and road racers are world famous for their bed time abilities and conquests but just why did Barry carry on the way he did when he was so famous and married to Stephanie? I have no doubt he loved her and was committed to their relationship, but he lived dangerously and I cannot see the real benefit. It was Paul Newman the famous and stunningly good looking Hollywood superstar who said 'I have steak at home why would I go out for a burger'. When it comes to steak Stephanie was unbeatable surely. I mean if you need a burger as well then you have an issue matey. And I sort of think that sums it up. Barry was either a sex pest or addicted to it or had that boyish relationship with girls and their tits in that he couldn't resist. But it got him into trouble and may well have resulted in accusations in recent times had he still been with us.

Here's what happened allegedly in Australia some years ago with his old mate Gerhard Berger of the Ferrari persuasion.

This from the internet but it was widely reported around the world at the time:

Race ace Gerhard Berger has admitted going into a public toilet to have sex with a pretty teenager.

*He has told police that 19-year-old blonde Melanie Hilzinger showed her breasts to him and former world motor-cycle champion **Barry Sheene**.*

*But the Austrian motor-racing star denies exposing himself and making Melanie into a "sex sandwich" with **Sheene**. His police statement says neither he nor **Sheene** touched her in a sexual way and she was allowed to leave when she wanted.*

*The encounter took place on March 1 in a toilet for the disabled at Broadbeach, Queensland, as 36-year-old Berger prepared for the Australian Grand Prix. Shop assistant Melanie claims **Sheene** pulled up her white top to expose her breasts and she was groped as she was wedged between the men. She says Berger dropped his pants and sucked her nipples.*

Berger, who married Portuguese ex-model Ana-Marie Corvo last September, was questioned by police.

***Sheene**, 46, who has lived in Australia with his ex-model wife Stephanie since 1987, was also quizzed and denies Melanie's allegations. Both men are expected to be charged with indecent assault.*

Berger lives in Monte Carlo and can't be forced to return to Australia.

But he could be arrested if he returns voluntarily at any time.

*Melanie was invited to lunch with the two track stars at the Pacific Fair shopping mall. She claims **Sheene** got her into the toilet by saying he was going to play a prank on his pal.*

*She went to the police after her boyfriend Kevin told her she "shouldn't let them get away with it." Berger says he believed the girl wanted to have sex with him and **Sheene**, but once inside the toilet she changed her mind. An extract from his statement, shown on Australian TV, said the men "did not touch the complainant in a sexual manner or in any other way."*

Berger dated a string of beauties before his marriage. The millionaire playboy vowed to end his nightclubbing days after his former McLaren team-mate Ayrton Senna was killed in a crash two years ago.

Ok so in the end the charges were dropped and this all faded from view but as far as I remember this wasn't the first time Berger and Barry were involved in some sexual high jinx. I cannot find reference to it now and thus I could be wrong, but I seem to remember the pair of them being interviewed at either the German or Austrian Formula One GP for a similar party piece involving a girl and the toilets inside the circuit. And even if they weren't questioned over this event Berger was known to have said he and Barry got up to naughty boy stuff several times. So why would Barry risk his marriage and reputation for a quick fondle or illicit bunk up? I don't know for sure but would guess it's because of opportunity and the feeling that he was secure and safe due to his fame, and that Stephanie wouldn't leave him.

So let's get into one of the rumours that had the most traction with us on the inside of the paddock at the time of Barry's wedding to Stephanie. Have you ever seen a picture or heard any report about the wedding of Barry and Stephanie? Probably not because as far as I am aware there was just one picture taken and the wedding was attended only by Barry,

Stephanie and Barry's parents Frank and Iris. I am not sure even where it took place but it was on February 16th 1984. So the story goes that the wedding was hastily organised by Stephanie because something significant and distasteful had happened just days before. It was so low key that even best mate Steve Parish wasn't there. Out of season it was Barry's Sunday morning routine to have breakfast and then while Stephanie was beginning to start the Sunday lunch he would go into town for the papers and then on to Gatwick to check his helicopter over. He loved his helicopter and so why wouldn't he want to admire the looks and curves of such a wonderful machine. But that wasn't all he was admiring. According to the rumour, which makes sense to me but obviously I cannot verify, he was regularly seeing or seeing to a British Airways or British Caledonian air hostess on the back seat of his helicopter. On this particular morning Stephanie had been alerted to something being odd with Barry or maybe she had been told of what was happening. She waited for Barry to leave and then after half an hour or so went to the hanger at Gatwick where Barry's chopper was parked. She found them at it, dragged him out and told him he had a few days to sort out the wedding licence and paperwork or she would go to The Sun newspaper and ruin his reputation and then she would leave him too. Hence the immediate wedding, no reporting and few if any pictures. I have to say this story came from someone very close to Barry a few years after the event. Someone almost unimpeachable. It makes sense and I am inclined to believe it.

But it didn't stop there because he was at it in Australia too. A former Suzuki rider told me that while he was racing